LIFE AND TIMES
OF THE
Falls Church News-Press

CHARLIE CLARK

THE
History
PRESS

Published by The History Press
Charleston, SC
www.historypress.com

Copyright © 2023 by Charlie Clark
All rights reserved

Front cover: The Falls Church City Council chamber was packed with readers of a *News-Press* "Extra" on a 1992 special election to fill a state delegate seat, and (*top*) a crowd of readers at the 1993 Memorial Day parade. *From the News-Press.*
Back cover: Music fans line up at the Little City's iconic, restored State Theatre. *Gary Mester.*

First published 2023

Manufactured in the United States

ISBN 9781467155328

Library of Congress Control Number: 2023938435

To all my charming neighbors.

Contents

Acknowledgements

Many thanks to past *News-Press* staffers Patricia Blystone, Julie Day, Jackie Droujinsky, Paul Donio, Peg Jones, Jenny Edwards, Bill Johnson, Joe Driver, Paul Greenberg, Brian Boyle, Vicki Rhoden, Teddy Wiant, Nathan Hamme, Joel Hardi, Isaac Blake, Jason Motlagh, Michael Cary, Adam Chandler, Beau Fay, James Tatum, Chris Geurtsen, Sean Nannery, Dan Arnaudo, Paul Arnaudo, Andrew Goetting, Eric Jacobs, Mo Sadeghi, Alaina Sadick, Josh Singer, Sean Snider, David Sprankle, John Humphries and his sons David and Robbie, Drew Maier and Nate Taylor. Thanks also to Natalie Bedell, Jonathan Harper, Dean Edwards, Mike Hume, Darien Bates, Peter Laub, Diana Glazer, Eamonn Rockwell, Nancy Davis, Danielle Manigault, Joe Fridling, Donna Talla, Scott Greene, Lou Emery, Roberto Flores, Deborah Smyth, Marilyn Austin, Helen Walters, Drew Costley, Jody Fellows, Leslie Poster, Matt Delaney, Amanda Snead, Orrin Kronheim, Alex Russell, Melissa Moore, Nick Gatz (longtime designer, advertisement salesman and managing editor), Ted White, Julio Idrobo, Kylee Toland, Brian Reach and Sam Mostow.

Thanks to the staff from the Mary Riley Styles Library, Olga Kesenko, Beth Meadows, Marshall Webster, Catherine Wilson; photograph consultants Jane Martin, Gary Mester, Josh Brick, Design Frames and Tony Awad of Photoscope; and history consultants Keith Thurston and Marybeth Connelly.

INTRODUCTION

How best to follow the goings-on in Northern Virginia's Little City? Since 1991, readers have imbibed the weekly tabloid bearing the Gothic nameplate of the *Falls Church News-Press*. Home-delivered, updated online and scattered at sites around the suburb of the nation's capital, the free paper knits together the hometown of 14,658 souls of varying philosophical leanings, who inhabit a dynamic place that doubles as an intimate village of 2.11 square miles. Falls Church City is ringed by a larger market of readers, advertisers and businesses on the edges of neighboring (and mammoth) Fairfax County. Falls Church schools own some Fairfax land, while shrimp-sized Arlington County shares with Falls Church its court system, jail and firefighters. Fairfax occasionally appears to bully the Little City, fighting it for years over the city's profit rates from owning part of the larger county's water supply. A *News-Press* editorial likened it to "the range wars of the Wild West." (That clash was finally settled after a 2013 referendum for a sale of water to Fairfax for land and reserve funds for Falls Church.)

Looking back now, in 2023, it's been three decades since a full history of Falls Church was published, roughly the same period occupied by the *News-Press*. And it is through that newspaper's eyes that this book portrays the Little City in its glory and frailties. Its founder, Nicholas F. Benton, is a native Californian, college baseball player, degreed master of divinity, gay activist and journalist born "with printer's ink in his veins"—or so he suspects. He launched the *Falls Church News-Press* largely as a one-man band. But with unflagging energy, he emerged as a major influencer and talent nurturer.

Modern welcome signs reinforce the identity of Falls Church. *Author's photograph.*

Benton knows the key players, hosts frequent parties and can be seen walking the streets and dining at eateries that make Falls Church homey.

In editorials (written every week by Benton himself), the editor strives to protect the city's prize schools by pressing for property tax revenues and favoring development in the occasional battles with traditionalists who treasure the residential village. He made his mark on zoning disputes over how to tastefully attract commercial development. *News-Press* news sections combine small-town intimate coverage—plenty of photographs of smiling residents lined up for the camera—with exclusive accounts of action by the city council and school board (at whose meetings Benton is sometimes the only member of the audience). Alongside these articles appear sophisticated essays on overseas wars and authoritative columns by state and federal lawmakers. Because Falls Church's demographics include a bevy of federal employees and, more recently, technology specialists, the *News-Press* offers highbrow commentary supplemented by syndicated columns from the *New York Times*. The editor shepherded this paper through the news media's transition to a round-the-clock digital environment.

Some say it's a miracle that Benton's close-to-home news organ—backed neither by inherited wealth nor corporate investors—has survived three decades, given the current death knells for local news outlets.

Since 2005, more than one-fourth of the nearly 9,000 U.S. newspapers (mostly weeklies) have folded, due either to declining subscriptions, internet competition for advertisements or acquisitions by (sometimes) predatory corporate chains, according to ongoing research at Northwestern University's Medill School of Journalism. More than 360 publications bit the dust during the COVID pandemic, between late 2019 and May 2022, leaving about 1,230 dailies and 5,150 weeklies publishing.

The book you hold relays the tale of how Benton pulled things off. His secrets? He takes virtually no vacations (beyond a few weekends). He pays staff writers (and offers health insurance) rather than engaging too many volunteers. He hires and mentors high school students. He gives the paper out for free and publishes letters that criticize. He donates to charities and cultivates youth readers by boosting high school and Little League sports, holiday parades, scouting and local history. His team covers charities, efforts to aid the homeless, published authors, theater productions, demands for low-income housing, struggling small businesses, gay rights and wars over parking. And Benton invites the public to his office parties.

But this book is also a primer on the colorful entity of Falls Church. It was named in the eighteenth century for a nearly three-centuries-old Episcopal church, where George Washington and George Mason were vestrymen. During the Civil War, it was an important crossroads to the battlefields. It made twentieth-century history in 1915, with the founding of the nation's first rural branch of the NAACP. And in the 1990s, it welcomed the Eden Center, the East Coast's largest Asian marketplace. What is officially nicknamed the Little City was dubbed a Tree City USA four decades ago by the National Arbor Day Foundation. In 1966, the city merited a sly mention by Mama Cass of the pop group the Mamas and the Papas in their version of the soul classic "Dancing in the Street." (Those local streets handle forty thousand pass-through cars daily.) And in 2007, Falls Church was named the "Harry-est town in America" by Amazon for the most online advance purchases of J.K. Rowling's *Harry Potter and the Deathly Hallows*. The city is known statewide for its extensions of the University of Virginia and Virginia Tech. Lesser known is that fact that it boasts two recording studios, four musical instruments stores, a prestige concert venue, two community theaters and, soon, a coming multiscreen movie theater.

Falls Churchians are unsure their town has a center. Given the shifting development activity, the town square could be the ancient intersection of Washington and Broad Streets, the Cherry Hill Park and community center near city hall and the Civil War–era farmhouse, or perhaps the new commercial development called Founders Row at West Broad and West Streets. "Just what is Falls Church? Or who is Falls Church?" asked Barbara Gordon, writing in the *News-Press* in August 2000 as the executive director of the Falls Church Chamber of Commerce. "Some might say it's a state of mind. Others would counter; it's a state of confusion." It's also a community of contrasts, from the long-gone Davis Gun Shop on South Washington Street to the subsidized townhomes for seniors at Winter Hill, just blocks from the upscale and historic homes that line Hillwood and Cherry Streets.

The newspaper's decades track society's changes—it covered the arrival of video rental stores and then covered their demise. And it stoked historical discussions, great and small. (Did President Herbert Hoover ever visit Falls Church? Yes, said a letter published in February 1997, when he was commerce secretary.)

Your narrator is one step removed as the *News-Press*'s "Our Man in Arlington" columnist for the past dozen years. I hang my hat just across the border. But in childhood, I patronized Falls Church's State Theatre for movies and concerts, the Village House Skating Rink (now Kaiser Permanente), the old Hechinger's Hardware, Giant Music for records and, later, Syms (now a 24 Hour Fitness) for tuxedos. As an adult, I still frequent the town's restaurants, furniture repair shops, office suppliers and car wash. My regular lunches with those who were once called "ink-stained wretches" on the newspaper staff assemble many plugged-in citizens (invited by Benton). They make this ringer feel like one of the gang.

"The *News-Press* is one of the things that make Falls Church special," Mayor Dave Tarter told me as this book was in preparation. "The paper reinforces and enhances the sense of community of shared experiences" in covering stories that the *Washington Post* would not make space for. "It is a labor of love for Nick Benton, and it shows. Whether you love it or hate it, everyone reads the *News-Press*."

1
ESSENTIALS OF LITTLE CITY HISTORY

The last time a history of Falls Church was published was 2012, with Cathy Taylor's photograph assemblage in *Historic Falls Church* (Arcadia Publishing). It followed *Victorian Falls Church* (2007) in Arcadia's Images of America series, which was assembled by the Village Preservation and Improvement Society and the staff at the Mary Riley Styles Library. Before that, library history consultant Bradley Gernand, in 2002, published *A Virginia Village Goes to War: Falls Church During the Civil War* with Doning Co. Publishers. In 2000, Gernard teamed up with prominent Northern Virginia historian Nan Netherton to release *Falls Church: A Virginia Village Revisited*, also with Doning Co. (with a foreword by Mayor David Snyder). All were given splashy coverage in the *News-Press*. The exception is the granddaddy of them all: the 1964 hardback volume by Methodist minister Melvin Steadman Jr., titled *Falls Church: By Fence and Fireside*. It is rich in early regional history and includes key family trees.

Proof that the Little City has a deep past shows up in the continuing work by the Village Preservation and Improvement Society. Its volunteers have tended shared spaces and read the nation's founding documents in public on July 4. Its revitalized modern incarnation promotes healthy trees, bestows architectural awards and sponsors concerts in Cherry Hill Park.

The city's official Historical Commission gives the local government material on historical matters, develops ways to identify historic buildings and sites and makes recommendations for recognizing them. Its five volunteers display city history documents and artifacts while advising the city

Union troops gathered at Falls Church Episcopal during the Civil War. *Metropolitan Museum of Art, Harris Brisbane Dick Fund, 1933.*

In 1896, Brown's Hardware—opened in 1883 and still operating—survived a burglar's attempt to blow up its safe. *City of Falls Church.*

council, city manager, Falls Church Planning Commission and Architectural Advisory Board.

Since 1997, Falls Church has been home to the Tinner Hill Heritage Foundation, a volunteer group that preserves early civil rights history. It is named for the hill off South Washington Street that was once the home of Joseph Tinner, the site of the creation of the NAACP's first rural branch in 1915. Its volunteers promote an understanding of city residents' role in the post–Civil War Jim Crow era through the 1950s and 1960s civil rights movement. Its visible projects include the curved stone monument on South Washington Street and nearby public art and the staging of the annual Tinner Hill Music Festival.

Also active is the Women's History Group, which organizes an annual women's walk around the city. There's a military forum that was formed in 1981 for history talks and veterans' groups that march in parades and bring costumed reenactors together for a Civil War Remembrance Day. In October 1999, as the *News-Press* reported seriatim, the city marked its tercentennial. Among the events was activist Barbara Cram's presentation for the chamber of commerce marking the history of Brown's Hardware, which, since 1883, had been operating at the city's main intersection. Current proprietor Hugh Brown was commended by Mayor David Snyder, and tales were told of founder J.W. Brown, who died in 1904, being victimized when robbers tried to blow up his safe in 1896.

Key Events in Falls Church History

1699
The area that became Falls Church was, for millennia, occupied by American Indians before the English settlement, dated by a cabin engraved with the year.

1732
The Virginia Colonial Assembly establishes Truro Parish for the Anglican Church. Once construction was completed in 1734, and the church was eventually named for "the falls" on the Potomac River, above what is now Chain Bridge.

1748
George Mason, a Fairfax County plantation owner and thinker behind the Bill of Rights, is made vestryman at the Falls Church.

1763
George Washington and George William Fairfax are appointed church wardens. A contract for a new brick building is accepted by local architect James Wren.

1809
The Leesburg Turnpike Company is established by the General Assembly to construct a road (now Route 7) from Leesburg to Alexandria.

1814
President James Madison comes to Wren's Tavern in Falls Church during his escape from the British troops during the War of 1812.

1824
Revolutionary War hero Marquis de Lafayette stops at Falls Church's Big Chimneys home (built in 1699) during his grand tour of America.

1831
The Mount Hope farm is built on the town's earliest mail route and is the oldest surviving Falls Church residence.

1845
A Greek Revival farmhouse called Cherry Hill is built, and a barn is added eleven years later.

1852
Falls Church is linked to the District of Columbia via a road from Georgetown's Aqueduct Bridge (roughly today's Wilson Boulevard).

1856
Columbia Baptist Church is founded by abolitionists.

1859
The railroad arrives in Falls Church, establishing its role as a regional crossroads.

1861
The Civil War Battle of Munson's Hill occurs near today's Bailey's Crossroads. The Union defensive Fort Buffalo is built at Seven Corners.

The history trail's entrance near Cherry Hill Park forms part of its Civil War walking route. *Author's photograph.*

1861
Thaddeus Lowe flies first balloon for warfare at Taylor's Tavern (today's Koons Ford) to surveil Confederate troops.

1864
Confederate major John Mosby conducts nighttime raids on Falls Church, and the church is used as a Union hospital.

1869
Dulin Methodist Church is founded.

1875
Falls Church petitions to become a Virginia township within Fairfax County after a debate on schools, temperance and segregation.

1882
The town council appoints a school committee led by Joseph Riley, resulting in the construction of the Jefferson Institute in 1882.

1883

Brown's Hardware is founded (still operating) at West Broad and Washington Streets.

1885

The Falls Church Improvement Society is founded.

1888

The railroad is formalized. Renamed the Washington, Arlington and Falls Church Railway in 1904, it later becomes the W&OD.

1908–14

Big Chimneys is demolished.

1910

Summerfield Taylor's Market and Apothecary opens near East Broad and Washington Streets.

1915

An African American group objects to a racial segregation ordinance and forms the first rural branch of the NAACP.

1922

Lee Highway is constructed as a modern paved road for cars from Southwest Virginia to Washington, D.C.

1936

Falls Church loses a court case, and the East Falls Church neighborhood becomes part of Arlington.

1945

Falls Church High School (Fairfax County) is founded.

1948

Falls Church incorporates as a city to secure the school district.

Big Chimneys in the early twentieth century. It is now a park. *Mary Riley Styles Library.*

1952
George Mason Junior and Senior High School is founded (renamed Meridian High School in 2020).

1961
Falls Church City Public Schools begin integration.

Late 1960s
Falls Churchians protest plans for Interstate 66 to bisect the city. The road is rerouted before its opening in 1982.

1991
The *Falls Church News-Press* is founded.

1999
A yearlong celebration of the city's tercentennial begins with the Watch Night New Year's Eve celebration tradition.

Unsurprisingly, the *News-Press* is not the Little City's first newspaper. An eight-page broadsheet called the *Falls Church Echo* debuted in October 1940, "locally owned" by editor and publisher C.G. Manley for a "rapidly growing city" that needed more than the Washington-based papers. From his office at 118 East Broad Street, Manley charged five cents for the weekly publication every Friday. The November 13, 1946 issue reported that Colonel Fenwick (no first name needed) was elected the Democratic Party leader in Falls Church. The Crossman Church celebrated its seventieth anniversary, and the newly formed adult football team, the Falls Church Independents, beat the Mount Ranier Ramblers 13–6. The paper also ran a photograph of the Madison School fourth graders and national comic strips such as Milton Caniff's *Terry and the Pirates*. In a precursor to modern-day dust-ups, a headline ran: "Keith Denied Rezoning After Public Protests." A builder named James Keith wanted to construct garden-type apartments for sixty families at 201 Great Falls Street using spot zoning. But forty residents signed a petition to block him, so the planning commission recommended against it. In yet another foreshadowing of the *News-Press*'s role, the issue for December 6, 1946, announced, "Business Men Unite in Chamber of Commerce." The *Echo* died in the early 1950s.

Then came the *Falls Church Standard*, part of a local King Publishing Co. and edited by Margaret King. It endured from 1953 to 1959. The year 1965

A *News-Press* predecessor called the *Echo* was published from 1940 to the early '50s. *Mary Riley Styles Library, author's photograph.*

brought another regional chain's offering: the *Falls Church Globe* announced it was "covering the City of Falls Church and Fairfax County." Copies by mail or courier cost ten cents, or four dollars per year, and readers were asked to submit a printed coupon. It published news you can use on voter registration or bicycle license plates. "Council Defers Action on Beautification," said one familiar-sounding headline, along with "High School Teachers Study Problems at George Mason." Local twelve-year-old junior ice skater Dawn Glab of 2351 Meridian Street was profiled as the Pacific Coast junior ladies skating champion.

From July 1975 to March 1977, city readers picked up the *Sound of Falls Church*, a twenty-four-page monthly (for three dollars a year) published by Dan Curran. It covered the dedication of the renovated Cherry Hill farmhouse.

And finally, in 1982, came the sophisticated *Falls Church News-Advertiser* (named for a similar paper launched in 1878), billed as "Falls Church's Community Newspaper," later "Your Community Newspaper" and, still later, "An Independent Newspaper." Editor and publisher David Pilvelait had a masthead listing only three staffers and no reporters. The first issue of the tabloid, dated January 21–28, 1982, was sold for fifteen cents and rose to a circulation of twenty thousand in Falls Church, McLean, Fairfax and North Arlington. It ran cartoons by the world-famous Pat Oliphant. An editorial endorsed Frank Wolf for the U.S. Congress and ran a full-page advertisement for Republican delegate Vince Callahan. The October 14, 1982 issue shouted, "We're Rich! According to the Census." Alas, after less than a year, in the final issue in December 1982, Pivelait wrote, "It is with sincere regret that this issue of the *News-Advertiser* will be the last. After four somewhat unsettled years of trying to establish a truly community-oriented newspaper for the Falls Church area, we have simply exhausted our resources of capital necessary to continue. We have averaged losses of nearly $10,000 per month for past six months."

The essentials of Falls Church history, of course, can be delivered in many ways. The city council, in January 1997, voted 7–0 to establish a Falls Church historic walking trail to unite the metal historic signs created post–World War II. The Little City now boasts two outdoor displays. On the sidewalk at Tinner Hill on South Washington Street (outside of 455 at Tinner Hill Apartments) lies a ground-level timeline of civil rights events and notable people going back three centuries. Installed in 2016, it reminds pedestrians of the area's African American educators, physicians, farmers, ministers, soldiers, artists and craftspeople.

And in October 2022, the village's broader history was encapsulated on eight illustrated standup panels at South Washington Street and Hillwood Avenue. Chronologically—starting in the 1600s—they were installed strategically by city communications staff "at a transportation hub for both residents and non-residents."

Historically, the Little City has boasted idiosyncrasies. Harry Fellows (1866–1943), for example, a U.S. Treasury tax specialist, was the mayor of Falls Church in the 1920s and is credited with helping sell the bonds that built the Madison Elementary School. During the 1920s, residents of the East Falls Church neighborhood (where Fellows lived on Washington Boulevard) complained of high taxes and poor water lines. They petitioned to leave the Little City and secede to Arlington. (There was already plenty of cross-border overlap: farmer Isaac Crossman, for whom a modern park and church are named, was a Falls Church elder, while his son George Crossman farmed from a home that is still occupied on what is Arlington's North Underwood Street.) After years of litigation, the secessionists won, and during that fight, in 1932, Fellows was elected as the first chairman of Arlington's new county board. History is always broadening, of course. In August 1999, the *News-*

The city erected streetside panels to present phases of its history in October 2022. *From the* News-Press.

Press published a photograph of Boy Scouts Patrick Starr and Matt Jackson after they found a Civil War bullet at Big Chimneys Park.

Falls Church was also once home to a boy who became one of the nation's most admired humorists, author James Thurber (a street bears his name). Soon after the *News-Press* launched, editor Benton, in February 1992, republished a 1967 *Saturday Evening Post* article explaining how Thurber, who lived here in 1902 as a six-year-old while his father worked at the State Department, lost an eye while playing bows and arrows with his brother.

Falls Church's grittier history gets mentioned in the *News-Press*. In December 2001, Benton quoted a *Newsweek* article in reporting that the city "had a bordello or two of its own in the past." In the 1970s, there were a dozen massage parlors, which gained national notoriety until "licensing and inspections drove them away." (By 2002, they were back, so the city council ended the legal ban, stepping up licensing.) The city also evolved from a southern, segregated, blue-collar town to the affluent, cosmopolitan, suburban village it is today.

And as many *News-Press* readers know, our current understanding of history is eternally changing. In August 2020, the Historical Commission recommended that the planning commission remove a plaque commemorating "the hanging tree." For much of the twentieth century, Falls Churchians had been told that Confederate major John Mosby had hanged captured Union soldiers from a high oak tree at the corner of West Broad Street and Virginia Avenue. Though the tree was felled in 1968, the city erected a plaque on the "hanging tree." But decades later, city researchers (Gernand among them) cast doubt, noting that Mosby did hang an abolitionist named John Read near that site. There was no evidence, however, that this was the tree, and twenty-first-century history specialists criticized the plaque as "a taunt" that brought to mind lynchings. The *News-Press* initiated the removal in an editorial, and Falls Church history marched on.

2
WHAT MADE BENTON A NEWSPAPER GUY

To create and run—in some weeks, single-handedly—the *Falls Church News-Press* required the background of a nick of all trades. His qualifications combined those of a business executive, hiring manager, wordsmith, commentator, policy analyst, athlete, pop music fan, theater critic, theologian and gay activist. And incidentally, he can report accurately and insightfully on taxes, budgets, development, education and politics.

Nicholas F. Benton was born on February 9, 1944, in Ross, California, north of San Francisco. His father, Ted, was a commercial deep-sea diver, and his mother, Jeanne, was a homemaker. (The two had been childhood sweethearts, though Nick would later portray his father as a bit of a tyrant.) He was raised in Santa Barbara, the middle child between his older brother, Stephen, and younger brother, Christopher. He attended elementary school in a two-room schoolhouse.

Benton published his first newspaper at the age of eight. The boy executed not just the writing of the *Benton Star* but the headlines and layout. With his mother's help, he acquired a 1940s hectograph gelatin sheet printer, similar to a mimeograph, that could spit out ten copies before the ink began fading. He sold them to neighbors for a dime each. As a prodigy in the memory department, young Benton also made a point of memorizing the names of all the U.S. presidents.

By the ninth grade, in 1959, Nick had founded a newspaper for his homeroom. He moved up to edit the *King's Page* weekly for 1,200 schoolmates at San Marcos High School in Santa Barbara. During his sophomore year, he began freelancing, covering hard news and sports for the local *Santa Barbara News-Press* (Does that name sound familiar?). That led to Nick's editorship of the student newspaper at Westmont College, a nearby private Christian school, from which he would graduate with an English degree in 1965. In the road-not-taken department, Benton was also showing promise on the baseball field, playing for Santa Barbara City College and the Goleta Merchant's semiprofessional team. A scout, after watching the teenage Benton hit a ball over the right field wall, offered a professional contract in the Dodgers farm system. But in those heady days of the early 1960s, Nick chose to play for Westmount on scholarship. (The baseball contacts he made would pay off in access to players as a reporter.)

Benton enrolled at the Pacific School of Religion in Berkeley (class of 1969). This brought him to the University of California's flagship school at the height of the antiwar, civil rights and student power protests, a time when the smell of the national guardsmen's tear gas was familiar on campus. Benton was awarded his master of divinity diploma *cum laude* on June 13, 1969 (it is framed and displayed today in the *News-Press* office). He worked as a youth minister for three years at seminary but never pursued that as a career. He would later consider his newspaper ownership a close substitute to ministry.

Benton remained in the Bay Area and worked for the famous alternative weekly the *Berkeley Barb*. Enjoying the freedom to publish on counterculture subjects from women's liberation to rock music, Nick, in 1971, landed an interview with Irish singing sensation Van Morrison. As he would proudly recall in the *News-Press*, Benton chanced to tell the singer-songwriter of his hitchhiking adventure back east that ended with Nick catching the tail end of Van Morrison's concert in a gym at the University of Buffalo. Soon after, Morrison released his album titled *Saint Dominic's Preview*, which includes the lyric: "Well, it's a long way to Buffalo and a long way to Belfast City, too."

While at the *Barb*, Benton also came out as gay, just before the 1969 Stonewall Riot in New York's Greenwich Village that launched the gay rights movement. His articles, he later wrote, "promoted the notion that fully actualized, gay liberation had the potential to be socially transformative." He also penned the editorial for the first edition of the *Gay Sunshine* newspaper, and he coproduced a pair of issues of his own fledgling gay newspaper, the *Effeminist*. Though in later years Benton would marry two women (his former wife Janine remains a close friend of his and an attorney for the *News-Press*), he would not come out as a gay advocate in mainstream publishing until the turn of the twenty-first century.

Benton's coming out in his twenties did not sit well with his family. "It was Christmas Eve 1970," he recalled in a memoir, "and when I arrived home by bus from San Francisco to our family home on the Southern California coast, I had long hair and a beard, and my father didn't need to know anything more than that." Nick was banished from the holiday dinner, where both his parents, his brothers and their wives had gathered, leaving him feeling "isolated and excluded."

Fearing his father's physical strength, Nick barged in on the meal and "unleashed a stream of loud, angry invectives" against his father. "So, you want to ruin our dinner?" the older man said from his chair. Nick stormed out but was pursued by his emotionally torn brothers. "I viewed that night as my coming out, claiming my integrity and my life and freeing me to become whatever life had in store," he later wrote. "Never again would I kowtow to unreasonable convention or fear." Later, he mellowed. "My father died in 2002, and toward the end of his life, we became close, and I respected, loved and helped him."

In mainstream politics, Benton, in 1972, backed the candidacy of Democrat George McGovern for president. But the South Dakotan war hero's landslide defeat by a Watergate-crimped Richard Nixon left Nick in search of alternative politics. "It was my own experience, as a late-1960s antiwar, pro–civil rights activist who came through a complicated maze to align with the then-socialist designs of one Lyn Marcus, a.k.a. Lyndon LaRouche," he would later write in the *News-Press*. "When I got involved with LaRouche, it was a different world," he explained. "The power of the antiwar and civil rights movements, propelled even more forcefully by reaction to the assassinations of Martin Luther King and Robert Kennedy, created a thirst and hope for a profound shift in society's fundamental values. But in the wake of the Nixon landslide, and estranged from my family because of my radicalism, I took a hard turn to the left."

Benton was warned by influences as notable as Representative Fortney Stark (D-California) that LaRouche was fishy, possibly a plant by the CIA or KGB. Still, Nick went to work organizing and reporting for the organization's *Executive Intelligence Review*. In the late 1970s, the group, while perhaps "well-meaning," Nick later wrote, revealed an ugly change that took years for Nick to recognize and detach from. Its "identity and practice shifted from being generally leftist to working with some of the most unsavory right-wing entities around," including anti-Semitic and antigay groups. As the group's "undernourished members 'deployed' for 16 hours a day raising money, and were forced to have, collectively, hundreds of abortions to save their

Old-school journalist Nick Benton laid out early issues using paste-up adhesive and X-ACTO knives. *From the* News-Press.

energies for serving him, LaRouche built up his ego, bully-lust, and palatial estate," Nick revealed in the *News-Press* in 2007. "I left that organization with extreme prejudice long ago."

By the 1980s, Benton's role with the *Executive Intelligence Report* had landed him in Washington, D.C., with a White House press pass. He soon knew it was time to change.

By October 1987, he had incorporated his own news service. A chance steer from a real estate agent prompted him, in November 1985, to quickly purchase a condominium on James Court in the suburb of Falls Church. (By coincidence, Falls Church was also where Benton's great-great-grandfather John Avery Benton, who fought with Sherman's Union army during the Civil War, stayed at the war's end, as recounted in a Nick Benton–penned biography.) Benton's news service incorporation became the context for "[his] decision in early December 1990 to launch the *News-Press*."

He would pull it off by charming volunteer labor and combining it with his own a seven-days-a-week style. Another secret to Nick's success: he is "frugal." There were no desks in the office, just boards and folding chairs.

"Editor in chief Nick Benton is too modest to blow his own horn," wrote reader Robert O. Beach in a letter published in March 1998. "But he deserves tremendous credit for the vital contribution the *News-Press* makes to our community."

On the central Falls Church question of revenue-producing real estate development, "Nick's role was pretty seminal," said Bob Young, one of the city's most active builders who, in 2023, was chairing its Economic Development Authority. "He very consistently backed responsible development but, at the same time, was not unwilling to criticize what he saw as irresponsible."

Environmental consultant and history activist Dave Eckert goes further. "The *News-Press* became the focal point of Falls Church," he said in 2022. "Nick Benton wanted to do good journalism, get readers and advertisements, but in many ways the paper brought the city together. And in many ways it drove it apart."

3

A Chancy Rollout

When Benton landed in Falls Church in November 1985, there was a news vacuum; residents depended on sporadic coverage in the *Washington Post*, the *Washington Times* and the suburban *Journal Newspaper* chain. In 1987, Benton attended the first-ever class in television production offered by the Falls Church Cable Access Corporation. There, he made a professional and personal friend out of a corporation board member and National Geographic Society writer named H. Robert "Bob" Morrison. (That Falls Churchian would soon win an election for Falls Church treasurer.) Together, Morrison and Benton produced the Falls Church Cable Access Corporation's first public access program, *Eye on Washington*, which went on to broadcast fifty half-hour editions on national politics. In the spring of 1990, Benton and local contacts produced the first *Election Night Live* show for the cable channel, giving the public swift firsthand results of the city council elections that May, including interviews with the candidates.

In late 1990, the city's then–Public Information Office director Barbara Gordon published a write-up of that May's *Election Night Live* in the city's monthly newsletter, the *Focus*. It was mailed to every city household. Benton took Gordon's *Focus* article as a cue to launch his newspaper. In early December 1990, he accepted invitations to speak before various groups and met with local leaders. The breakthrough came at that month's meeting of the board of directors of the Falls Church Chamber of Commerce. To Benton's surprise, the business board, at the initiative of executive director (and retired U.S. Navy commander) Robert S. "Hap" Day, voted

Chamber of commerce executive director Robert S. "Hap" Day gave the nascent newspaper a pivotal vote of confidence. *From the* News-Press.

unanimously that night to endorse the project. Day went on to join Benton's strongest supporters.

Next, Benton bought a mailing list of all the chamber members, about 230 labels. Singlehandedly, he stuffed envelopes with a cover letter and a stamped return postcard with two boxes to check, one indicating an interest in advertising should a newspaper be founded and another indicating no interest. The encouraging response: more than 60 percent of the postcards came back expressing an interest in advertising.

Benton showed those postcards to officers at the new local bank, which had a mandate to serve its community. Its president was on the chamber board. A line of credit of $25,000 was granted that allowed the purchase of one Dell 380 computer and a printer. Benton then set a firm date for the first issue: March 28, 1991. It was a chancy maneuver. The American economy's go-go years of the 1980s were downshifting—a recession lasted from July 1990 to March 1991—and Benton had no investors.

Then Benton made more connections among neighbors in the walkable Falls Church region. A key resource was Mike Diener, a CPA (and, later, the chamber of commerce president and a designated "Pillar of the Community") whom Benton met at a mixer. His accounting business became an early advertiser (continuing for three decades) and helped Benton set up his payroll—this was later farmed out and then brought in-house before being farmed out again. The two became lunch buddies. "The city was very political at the time," Diener recalled in 2022. It was dominated by "one party that was antibusiness." So, he and Benton teamed up on a strategy to "pound the message" that connected a healthy business community with increasing tax dollars to be spent improving schools.

Benton also roped in Danny O'Brien, a twenty-year-old "sidekick with no newspaper experience but a lot of enthusiasm and encouragement," who helped sell the first advertisements.

The name of the *Falls Church News-Press* was a tribute to Benton's boyhood hometown paper, the *Santa Barbara News-Press*, which dates to 1868 (but folded in 2023). He chose a classic Gothic nameplate and reproduced in every issue a seven-point editorial platform created by his hometown newspaper publisher T.M. Storke. The goals: keep the news clear and fair, play no favorites, never mix business and editorial policy, do not let the news columns reflect editorial comment, publish the news that is public property without fear or favor to friend or foe, accept no charity and ask no favors, give "value received" for every dollar you take in and make the paper show a profit if you can—but above all, keep it clean, fearless and fair.

The *News-Press* would cover city council and school board proceedings, budgets and taxes, commercial and residential development and crime. (Benton was careful in reprinting the police blotter to avoid using the names of alleged perpetrators unless they'd been convicted.) Add in youth sports, music and theater reviews, plus shared holiday celebrations, and you have a true community newspaper. Given the Little City's educated and sophisticated citizenry, Benton would combine small-town intimacy with highbrow opinion columns from office holders and syndicated commentators. He would publish reviews of restaurants and new small businesses—all potential advertisers. And in the first issue, he announced an advisory board for the Falls Church "paper of record." The well-placed professionals included: H. Robert Morrison (chair), Tom Clinton, Hap Day, Tom Gilliland, Dr. William Johnson, Robert H. Blanchard and Molly Henneberg.

Much of the copy was written by Benton himself (he would sometimes have three bylines on page 1), but he roped in part-time writers and volunteer scribes. A paid production staff being too expensive, Benton reverted to his high school days and executed the headlines, layouts and page-proof paste-up alone using an X-ACTO knife and adhesives that now seem quaint. He drove the flats to the printer.

"We worked all night on that first issue," Benton recalled, "and as the deadline approached, as dawn began to break on March 27, we looked out our second-story windows to see that the cherry blossom trees on North Virginia Avenue had blossomed overnight. That was our sign to press ahead!"

After the proverbial all-nighter, his team of three drove to Gaithersburg, Maryland, to the Comprint Co. plant to witness the maiden print run. "When the press bell rang and everything started to move, it was a very special moment," Benton remembered. "As the papers started chugging onto a conveyor belt, I couldn't help but stand on a box and loudly exclaim, 'Let every tyrant tremble!' The noise of the press drowned me out so that only a couple of pressmen gave me funny looks."

Back in Falls Church, young O'Brien had walked the streets crowing, "Have you heard the news? Come March 28, Falls Church is going to have its own newspaper!"

The only snafu was that Benton, as his team drove to the printer in his friend Bill Johnson's Mustang convertible, neglected to find a way to get the freshly bundled 7,500 copies back to the new distributor in Falls Church. Out in Maryland, they chanced on an entrepreneur who ferried papers for other organizations and made him a handsome cash offer to deliver the

"When the press bell rang and everything started to move, it was a very special moment," Benton recalled. *From the* News-Press.

bundles to Benton's first distributor, John Humphries, who was waiting in a Falls Church living room.

The trio returned home as the sun came up on March 28. The headline on the first issue: "Rancorous Public Hearing on School Cuts, Tax Increase." Later that day, after some sleep, Benton determined he would put out the second weekly edition. And he was off.

Financially, the publishing venture got off to a scary start. Benton, on one spring day, saw that he had only five dollars in the bank, and the printer, awaiting payment, reminded the entrepreneur that he was "not a bank." So, the editor-publisher assembled his bookkeeper, part-time reporters and distributor and promised them, "I can't pay you now, but I will." And he did. Benton proved himself a risk-taker. One of his earliest editorial stances required him to oppose, in the October 1, 1992 issue, a city referendum that would allow for local parimutuel horse race betting. As editorial content improved, so did circulation and advertisement sales. In the December 26, 1991 issue, city economic development coordinator Nicholas Moscatiello published a letter announcing, "It gives me great pleasure to inform you that the *Falls Church News-Press* has been chosen '1991 Business of the Year' by the City of Falls Church."

"If you respect someone, pay them at least a little" was Benton's approach to recruiting talent. Mike Hoover, a local educator, was recruited in 1991 for what became a decades-long role as a columnist. "Nick called to talk to Mr. Mike Hoover, [a] journalism teacher at George Mason High School," he recalled as a retiree in 2022.

> He didn't really want to talk to the journalism teacher as much as he wanted to get in touch with the possible pipeline to some eager, young, inexperienced, inexpensive (free even?!) young writers who might want to help on the nascent newspaper. I'm sure I wondered if he was sane, considering how many papers all over the country were folding everywhere one looked, including ones I had written for or tried to freelance for. But Benton convinced me he was in it for the long haul. I'm sure I asked whether he had inherited some Santa Barbara gold mine or something.

When the *News-Press* won an award from the Virginia Press Association, Hoover, a sponsor of the high school paper the *Lasso*, responded with an advertisement in the *News-Press*, saying, "Congratulations from the other newspaper in town." In 1998, the *News-Press* made the Media Honor Roll of the Virginia School Boards Association, having been nominated almost annually by the Falls Church School Board. And in 2001, the Virginia General Assembly passed a resolution congratulating the paper on its tenth anniversary for a "job well done."

It would become a family affair. Benton's ex-wife Janine Schollnick Benton became the paper's legal counsel, and her mother, a London Eastender named Eileen Hecht Levy, was an occasional columnist.

Jody Fellows, who was recruited as a high school student and eventually devoted nineteen years to the paper (including fifteen as managing editor), in 2022, recalled the predigital production technology—printouts, waxers, pasteboards and an old-school fax machine that received press releases, letters to the editor and classifieds that had to be typed out. "During my first entrance to the *News-Press*, I noticed that Nick smoked cigars with the music of Bob Dylan and Van Morrison in the background, so the entire office stank," he remembered. Fellows came to admire Benton's passion for "building up the paper and promoting it at every opportunity." It was ten years before Nick missed a Wednesday night (the final production time), as he came in, even when he felt sick.

The choppy waters calmed, and the paper's boat was righted, thanks to the wee-hours energy over the years from circulation distributors, including the paper's present-day distributor, Julio Idrobo. They used a combination of home delivery and 250 black metal and logo-bedecked boxes in highly trafficked areas. "Want your *News-Press* Mailed to You or a Loved One Who Lives Outside the City?" asked a 1992 house advertisement. It cost "$25 per year." Delivery by carrier has served every city household since the paper's launch.

Benton was a quick study on the heritage of longtime Falls Churchians. In the April 14, 1994 issue, he published a two-page spread titled "The Life and Times for Mr. Falls Church." Along with an editorial, he celebrated Donald Frady, the director of the Department of Public Works, who had died on April 12. With a park named for him, he was the force behind the first recreation center. "When we look at the community center, we look at the heart of Don Frady," the editorial said. He "helped transition Falls Church from a rural town to a thriving city." The all-important write-ups of community doings—weddings, graduations, job promotions—were handled by plugged-in "All About Falls Church" columnist Jackie Droujinsky.

The response from the city establishment became evident when the city council named the *Falls Church News-Press* "Business of the Year" again in 2001. Benton himself was named "Businessman of the Year" in 2007 and "Pillar of the Community" by the chamber of commerce in 1993 and 2003.

Benton wrestles with the first batch of his prized product to be rolled out in the community. *From the* News-Press.

Other milestones included the decision, in early 1995, to distribute boxes in North Arlington shopping centers, at the Arlington Courthouse and in downtown Washington, D.C., at the National Press Club and around Dupont Circle. In October 1996, with the press run growing from 8,000 to 10,000, the *News-Press* expanded door-to-door delivery for the first time beyond 2,000 outside the city. In May 1998, with circulation having risen to 12,000, the paper delivered to 9,000 households. Soon, with a 25 percent increase in circulation, the total of more than at 12,500 nearly matched the reach of the *Washington Post* in the Falls Church area and was nearly triple that of the Fairfax edition of the *Journal* newspapers (4,583). In October 2000, state delegate and columnist Bob Hull wrote a letter congratulating the *News-Press* on its five hundredth edition, declaring, "I know of no other newspaper that is so thoroughly read by so many people in the community to which it is circulated."

Editorially, there were hiccups. In late July 1996, the editor had to run a correction for having misattributed letters from James Longo and Debra Conley that were "submitted fraudulently by anonymous faxes." Describing the staff as "shocked and dismayed," the *News-Press* promised to check letters in the future and report any abuse to law enforcement. But in early August,

Benton had to run a "correction to the correction" after Longo came forward to stand by his letter. The staff was unable to confirm where Conley lived. In the May 26, 1994 issue, a reader complained of typos in a previous letter, noting that the key word *not* had been dropped in a discussion of alcohol abuse. And in January 1995, thieves struck: "Stacks of *News-Press* editions at locations around Falls Church were removed and copies of competitor or other free distribution newspapers were found in their place," said the report. Delegate Hull sought legislation to strengthen relevant penalties, and Benton testified in Richmond.

In 2001, Falls Church city manager Dan McKeever undertook a citywide survey asking where people got their local news. The results showed that, overwhelmingly, they relied on one of two sources: the *News-Press* or the city's own *Focus* newsletter. The drop-off of other sources was dramatic after that, including radio, TV (including Falls Church Cable) and internet sources. As a result, starting in July 2002, the city contracted to publish the *Focus* inside the *News-Press* each week, providing greater news and information than its newsletter could—and at a fraction of the cost. (That arrangement continued until 2008, when fiscal and political pressures on the city council killed it.)

By June 2003, circulation had climbed to twenty-three thousand, with deliveries going to every household in zip codes at 22041, 22042, 22043, 22044. At the start of that year, an editorial proclaimed 2003 "A Very Good Year" for the *News-Press*. Circulation rose to twenty-four thousand, with color advertisements that allowed more motifs to enliven layouts. Page counts rose from twenty-four to forty or forty-eight pages per issue.

Black metal distribution boxes were rolled out in April 2004, with an advertisement shouting, "So now, the *N-P* is even closer to you." (Newer boxes are green.) By the end of that year, a house advertisement began listing box locations, reading, "It's Thursday, Do You Know Where Your *News-Press* Is?" A house advertisement touted "Virginia's Progressive Newspaper." The coverage radius expanded to the Fairfax enclaves of Merrifield, Seven Corners and Dranesville and downtown to the Farragut West Metro. In November, Benton hired marketing experts for advertisement sales and the website, retaining Falls Church–based SmithGifford. The new slogan: "Local News, Global Perspective."

In February 2005, as the *Journal* newspapers ceased publication (their properties bought by the *Washington Examiner*), the *News-Press*'s circulation roared past thirty thousand. The surge continued, prompting a March 2, 2006 editorial saying Benton was "now grateful for the early skeptic who

Distribution boxes with the paper's logo became familiar sights in Falls Church and parts of Arlington, Fairfax and Washington, D.C. *Author's photograph.*

based a prediction on the snide comment "*if* the paper does make it to its one-year anniversary." The years in which Benton had "hammered away as a lonely prophet" had paid off. He would continue "championing affordable housing, equal rights and diversity, as well as providing a high-quality, popular local vehicle, otherwise unavailable, through effective, affordable advertising." The paper was "not being glib," the editorial proclaimed, "when we say this is how the *News-Press* supports family values."

In a November 1, 2007 editorial titled "20 Years My Own Boss," Benton marked the *News-Press* surpassing the *Washington Blade* circulation of 36,500 by taking staff to a lunch at the fancy Palm restaurant downtown. By this time, he had created a spinoff book publisher, BCI Books, which joined the weekly paper under the corporate entity Benton Communications. Between his news stories, editorials and national affairs column, launched in 1997, he personally was contributing three thousand to four thousand words per issue.

Thanks to an infusion of young staffers (the masthead total was never more than ten), the Little City newspaper kept pace with the digital revolution. It was in April 1997 that the city announced "citizens and business with access to the internet can now send E-mail messages to the city of Falls Church government at pcpio@erols.com." An advertisement announced that the first *News-Press* contribution to the fledgling World Wide Web was "Up & Running" at www.kreative.net/FCNP. The site was designed and maintained by Lucas Hardi (and later by high schoolers Paul Arnaudo and Alaina Sadick). By October 1998, house advertisements were inviting Falls Churchians to "Check out the *News-Press*, the *News-Press* live TV show, the 'White House Report' column, a Saturday city affairs broadcast on WFAX cable or AM radio at 1220" and, by the way, on the internet. Benton, in 1997, launched a TV segment "Tomorrow's *News-Press*" featuring himself and Hap Day to preview the coming edition. Along the way, Benton editorialized in a highly personal style that "a primary challenge for good community newspapers is to strive against the depersonalizing influences of the information revolution, in the many forms that impact the so-called mass media," he wrote in the May 25, 1995 issue. "It is only by confronting the need to reconcile differences with persons unlike one's self in shaping the destiny of a real community that persons have the potential to grow."

In June 2004, the *News-Press* began running separate email addresses for readers to communicate on general questions, delivery, classified advertisements, school news, letters to the editor, sports and the photograph feature called "Critter Corner." By March 2005, Benton was inviting feedback by including his personal email address in his general topics column.

The instant broadcasting capability of digital publishing allowed national and worldwide access, quick coverage of breaking news and the rapid correction of mistakes. But it had its downside: staff exhaustion,

This page: Accounting business owner Mike Diener (*right*) joined Benton in WFAX radio commentary before becoming a key advertiser, adviser and friend. *From the* News-Press, *author's photograph*.

for example, for those participating in the twenty-four-hour news cycle. And more important, the migration of readers from print to online news forced a new approach to advertising using the internet. Advertising profits dropped compared with old-fashioned print (particularly in classifieds, which were replaced by freebies on Craigslist). Audited circulation figures had to be recast and expressed as ten thousand copies printed and distributed, plus eighty thousand unique website visitors per month or eight hundred thousand unique hits on stories. Here's the pattern, based on *News-Press* reporting:

1991: 7,500 first press run
1995: 8,000
1996: 10,000
1998: 12,500
2001: 14,000
2002: 18,000
2003: 22,000
2004: 24,000
2005: 30,000
2006: 30,108
2007: 36,500 (the peak)
2023: 9,000 printed copies, 80,000 unique website visitors per month or 800,000 unique hits on stories

During that first banner year, 1991, Benton set up shop on the third floor of 105 North Virginia Avenue in the heart of the city. It was vital that readers, advertisers and those with news tips feel free to enter the office or communicate though fax, U.S. Mail and, later, email. Years later, Benton announced he had rented a larger office at 929 West Broad Street, Suite 200; then at 450 West Broad Street, Suite 321; and finally, he got an even better deal on rent at 200 Little Falls Road, Suite 310. The operation returned to a smaller space at 105 Virginia Avenue, Suite 310, in 2020. On all those office walls were displayed several general assembly proclamations honoring the newspaper; Benton on the cover of the Washington, D.C. gay-oriented, "metro" magazine *Citizen Nick*; and photographs of receptions in the offices, which brought in politicians, celebrity journalists and entertainers. The office holiday parties and pizza receptions that were open to the public were key to Benton's outreach. The events moved to larger digs, frequently the Center for Spiritual Enlightenment.

Talk of the Town: Bailey and Guggenmos' New Club, pg. 6

METROWEEKLY

AUGUST 9, 2007

Citizen Nick

Seeking Info in Wone Case, pg. 8
Houston, we've got a problem, pg. 34
Fallen *Stardust*, pg. 32

Nicholas Benton's gay-friendly, progressive paper grows in Falls Church

In 2007, Benton was the cover guy for a Washington, D.C.–based magazine focused on the gay community. *Author's photograph.*

Dave Eckert recalled attending the first party at Benton's "tiny office." "There was really just a handful of us there, all knew all, usual suspects," he said in 2022. "All of us were skeptical. None of us really knew Nick. He'd contacted us all. We could not believe that within one week, he was, like, the most important person in town. The newspaper was where people interested in Falls Church were going— immediately. Our mouths dropped. A lot happens in Falls Church, but it's hard to get something happening. It takes some real moxie. We were quite impressed with the first five editions: 'A Slugfest at City Hall.' It's ironic because no one would have ever heard about it" if not for the new *News-Press*.

Of course, not all residents were fans. Complaints charging bias or inaccuracy were dutifully printed in the *News-Press*, and doubtless, more were heard in private. On two occasions, news consumers banded together to publish an alternative. In May 1995, a respected city father named Edward Strait created the Falls Church Media Co. to launch the *Falls Church City Scope*, a free monthly. He promised in *Falls Church City Scope*, no. 1, to "promote the positive rewards of living, working, and doing business in Falls Church City." Also, the *Scope* would "protect and defend the independent cityhood of Falls Church City; advocate for a high-quality, independent school system; champion the cause of sound economic development in Falls Church City; and serve as an intermediary between the ordinary citizens of Falls Church and the business community." Its first issue celebrated the 1995 opening of the city's (still thriving) farmers' market at city hall. Welcoming letters to the publication were printed from then–Virginia governor George Allen, Lieutenant Governor Don Beyer, Delegate Bob Hull and the city's public-private partnership head William Baskin Jr. The *Scope*'s cover story, titled "Next Governor of Virginia," profiled hometown favorite Beyer and his wife, Megan. "Revitalization: 1996 Is Off to a Great Start" read a business story. A feature by Joan Lewis reflected on Founding Father George Mason (without mentioning slavery). And there were columns on gardening, food, health and teenage life.

Nate Martin (*left*) and Danny O'Brien (*right*) hawk the new *News-Press* at the Memorial Day parade. *From the* News-Press.

Interestingly, the *Scope* relied on the same advertisers the *News-Press* did, and at one point, Benton recalled, it offered to pool (or poach) his advertisements. The monthly lasted for ten issues.

Then in 2008, three parents in the school system launched an online "resource" called the *Falls Church Times*. Annette Hennessey, George Bromley and Scott Taylor promised continuously updated (or corrected) news and information pieces while maintaining nonprofit status. They said there would be "no personal attacks or mean-spiritedness" and a "willingness to publish opposing points of view" without political endorsements. Its volunteer editors and writers kept the *Times* going until 2017.

Benton chalks up the demise of his competition to a publication's need for a core staff that gets paid, even if many contributors are volunteers. He defends his admittedly unorthodox (in modern times) dual role as editor-publisher and political endorser while also serving (for two terms) as head of the chamber of commerce. "That was very common in past American history," Benton said, pointing to political activism in the nineteenth century by such loftier news industry personages as Horace Greeley, Joseph Pulitzer and William Randolph Hearst. Benton modeled himself on the local but national approach of the early twentieth-century luminary William Allen White, the editor-publisher of the *Emporia* (KS) *Gazette*.

In an August 2006 editorial titled "What Makes Us Tick," Benton idealistically defined the constituents of the *News-Press:* "Those who can't or don't, or buy a vote. It is the world's orphans and widows, too young or too old, dealt out of the mainstream calculus, cheated, shortchanged, abandoned, exploited, poor, hungry, ill, fodder for the aggression of the rich."

In the twenty-first century, Benton began supplementing revenues by offering *News-Press* "membership," which gave loyalists special content in return for annual donations in customized amounts. And in 2022, he introduced website readers to the E-edition, with its slogan: "It's the paper without the paper."

4

ADVERTISING FOR THE LITTLE CITY

The intimacy of Falls Church—where many institutions lie within walking distance of each other—creates a porous border between church and state, the common industry firewall between a publication's news and business sides.

So, when the *News-Press* covered openings of new retail outlets or reviewed area restaurants, it didn't fail to notice a potential advertiser.

It wasn't long after the paper's launch that it graduated from the noble-but-amateur advertisement sale efforts of young Danny O'Brien. A local named Andrew Turner, while he was in college preparing for a career as an international tax accountant, came aboard to help Benton send weekly bills to advertisers. (Part of the challenge was cajoling clients to submit their copy and visuals by press deadlines.) "Advertise in the *News-Press*: A local newspaper that supports local business, reaching a market that cares," read a house advertisement published on March 28, 1992. It offered advertisers who booked for fifty-two weeks their last four weeks free. The city and the legal community boosted the paper's revenues with regular agate-type mandatory public notices.

Soon, the *News-Press* would employ the first in a series of commissioned-based salespersons who were free to negotiate custom deals. Standard display advertisement rates, by 2022, were offered at $1,600 for full page, $130 for a two-by-two-inch section. In August 1993, a Virginia schoolteacher turned news entrepreneur named Gay Nuttall spoke to the chamber of commerce about an exciting new venture. The idea was to pool advertising regionally

An array of local advertisers became regulars in *News-Press* pages, some inspiring stories. *Author's photograph.*

among thirty-nine participating news dailies and weeklies. She wandered unannounced into the *News-Press* office at the urging of the then-publisher of the *McLean Providence-Journal.* She regaled Benton with a pitch on what became the Washington Suburban Press Network, a shared provider that would penetrate to 860,000 homes. The *News-Press*—along with neighboring papers, such as the Times Community Papers of Virginia and the Gazette papers in Maryland—would be outfitted with steady weekly advertising for national product brands and wide-release movies playing at area theaters. Over the next sixteen years, Nuttall traveled the lower forty-eight states to meet with corporate executives, advertising agencies and media buyer bigwigs in New York and Chicago. She grew the subscriber pool reach to 1.6 million.

"The secret to being a good salesperson," she told the *News-Press*, "is a willingness to keep beating your head against a wall, and discovering the wall begins to give. You must also believe you are doing it for a good cause." Nuttall later became the president of the Suburban Newspapers of America. She retired in 2008 (meriting a profile in the *News-Press*). Her properties were subsumed by the Reston, Virginia–based *Fairfax County Times*.

Another *News Press* advertising star was Blackwell Hawthorne, a politically conservative World War II veteran fighter pilot who made a dramatic, unannounced entrance through the office door. This senior citizen from Arlington was an experienced ad salesman but was a recent victim of digitization at his previous newspapers. The *Alexandria Connection* and the *Fairfax Journal* let him ago for his lack of computer skills. "He became the best advertising salesman we ever had," Benton wrote. Hawthorne made the *News-Press* fatter than ever, with issues thickening to forty-four and forty-eight pages. A parishioner at Falls Church Episcopal, he seldom saw eye to eye with the *News-Press* editorial line. But he was a hit at office parties, later thrilling the staff with his recounting, during two interviews with *News-Press* reporter Dean Edwards, of his exploits as a prisoner of war and an airman helping defeat Nazi Germany. "Blackie" sold advertisements through March 2009. He died at the age of eighty-seven in January 2010 and was buried at Falls Church's historic Oakwood Cemetery.

Display advertisements that became fixtures in the tabloid came from corporations, small businesses and political groups. The issue released on January 6, 1994, for example, showcased national chains Rite Aid and PetSmart, alongside a local business advertisement spreading the word about the SAID word processing and copy shop on West Broad Street. A house advertisement joined the chorus by proclaiming, "*News-Press* Advertisers Merit Your Support." A frequent early advertiser was Palestinian American Issa Khalil Ayoub, the proprietor of the popular Charlie's Pizza, whose untimely death in 1995 became a news story. Other regulars were dentists Mansour Mortazie and American Family Dental Care. In a subtle form of advertising, Benton, in July 1994, introduced a one-page directory of Falls Church businesses, charging five dollars per listing.

Veteran ad salesman Blackie Hawthorne, also a World War II veteran, reviews layouts with editorial assistant Drew Maier. *From the* News-Press.

In January 1995, the editor published a notice that, despite the printer's cost of newsprint having risen 5 percent, *News-Press* advertising rates wouldn't change until 1996. (Circumstances were different in June 2003, however. With circulation having doubled to twenty-four thousand, advertisement rates were raised 12 percent.) To mark his newspaper's anniversary, Benton editorialized in the March 30, 1995 issue that he was writing "with a special sense of joy and achievement that we enter our fifth year" and called relations with business community advertisers "mutually rewarding." An example of such mutual aid was the paper's nine-part series in the summer of 1996 chronicling the "Great Trans-America Bike Trip." Former staffer Nate Martin joined fellow teens Chris and John Yates and Rob Metcalf to cycle from Oregon to Virginia Beach, with visible sponsorship by the *News-Press*, Richmond Camera and Silver Diner.

By 1998, readers had become accustomed to standby advertisements from the local Point of View Eyewear Shop run by James Elkin. He praised *News-Press* advertisements, saying they "really work." Falls Church real estate superstar Merelyn Kaye, in the first issue, began a regular run of full-page advertisements showcasing photographs of all the homes she had either sold or was about to sell. And Anthony's Greek American restaurant began a series of *News-Press* advertisements that would halt and then continue after Anthony and Faye Yiannarakis were forced by development to close their restaurant (founded in 1972) at 309 West Broad. They later reopened at larger digs on nearby Annandale Road. In July 1999, a unique advertisement appeared for the historic Burke and Herbert with the message: "The OLDEST Bank in Virginia Is the NEWEST Bank in Falls Church." Perhaps the steadiest large advertiser over the decades has been the Don Beyer Volvo dealership, run by Congressman Beyer's brother Mike Beyer.

In the September 6, 2001 issue, cable TV giant Cox Communications took out a full page to express its thanks for its customers' patience during its regional system's $500 million upgrade. Reinforcing the importance of advertisements, Benton, in an April 8, 2004 editorial titled "We Are Family," stated that "the *News-Press*'s destiny has always been linked with the chamber of commerce" in its mutual goal of helping businesses and advertisers succeed.

The February 9, 2006 *News-Press* contained advertisements for prestigious merchants Tiffany's at Tyson's Corner and Bill Page Toyota, both in Fairfax. For Valentine's Day the following month, color advertisements allowed for a burst of pink and red fun with *News-Press* layouts.

In another sign of the paper's utility in branding, the city government itself, in late 2009, took out advertisements to showcase its own "brand name," the new and playful Little City logo.

Advertising revenues tended to rise, of course, during election seasons— that was April to May for local elections and September to November for state and national elections. In an October 1997 issue, Benton had to state a policy of capping the number of published letters endorsing candidates, lest they become "free ads." But full-page color advertisements from Democrats, Republicans and independents—local and statewide—enriched the paper's bottom line. In the fall of 2002, as Falls Church voters prepared to weigh in on a controversial referendum to alter the city charter to affect debates over development, loud advertisements were taken out by the chamber of commerce (against) and the Village Preservation and Improvement Society (in favor). Also appearing in the *News-Press* pages were advertisements from the highly capitalized Virginia Hospital Center (formerly Arlington Hospital). In 2013, the *News-Press* launched its annual "Restaurant Week" promotion, with participating advertisers including Applebee's, Argia's, Dogwood Tavern, Ireland's Four Provinces, the Mad Fox Brewing Company, Pizzeria Orso and Sfizi Café. When frequent advertiser Sisler's Stone lost its family executive Steve Sisler to retirement in August 2022, a *News-Press* profile presented the purveyor of natural stone as "hardworking, admired, team-oriented, innovative, loyal and beloved."

More personally, advertisements were taken out to express birthday greetings, and families of Falls Churchians who died young placed advertisements as tributes.

There was the steady run of house advertisements, which layout staff can use to make space adjustments. Early on, Benton invited supporters to send in ten dollars to have their name on a list in an advertisement wishing the *News-Press* a happy first birthday. Another in the April 23, 1998 issue offered an election-year six-month subscription for twenty dollars, alongside an offer of internships at the paper. "Get Noticed! Advertise in the *News-Press*!" read an in-house box in the June 16, 2006 issue. In 2010, house advertisements beckoned readers to "Write for the News-Press!" encouraging submissions as letters to the editor and guest commentaries. And by 2022, readers saw a house advertisement for "Books by Nicholas F. Benton," which include *Education of a Gay Soul*, *Gay Men in the Feminist Revolution* and *Extraordinary Hearts*.

Large revenues can come from small-type advertising. The classic newspaper section for classifieds over thirty-three years have played their role in creating *News-Press* community intimacy. The price in December 1993 was eighteen dollars per column inch, with a one-inch minimum, and a discount of twelve dollars was given for employment advertisements. An early success came in March that year, recorded in a front-page squib: "Cat Reunited With Owner Thanks to Classified Ad." The original notice had announced that "an all-black short-haired cat with yellow green eyes" had been found in the West Falls area. "We got only one call, but it was the right one," said the resident who placed the advertisement. By 1998, classified rates had risen to fifty cents a word. But in 1999, the structure was adjusted to allow twenty dollars for up to twenty words and then fifty cents were charged for each additional word—plus, you could add an attractive surrounding box for another ten dollars. In December 2004, the rate rose to sixty cents a word, and in August 2006, it was raised to sixty-five cents. In 2022, the price again came down to twenty dollars for up to twenty words and fifty cents for every word thereafter.

In both its advertisements and news columns, the *News-Press* became an outlet for the City of Falls Church to advertise itself. In December 2009, the SmithGifford firm unveiled to a citizen task force its design of a "brand name" city logo—an assignment initiated by the Falls Church Economic Development Authority. The dancing, colorful lettering embodied the Little

Some hosts of distribution points for the free paper keep previous issues on hand. *Author's photograph.*

City. Mayor Robin Gardner told the *News-Press* that the slogan and logo were "exciting." She said, "It captures the essence of the City of Falls Church. It is a tie that binds the city, its residents, its legacy, its innovation and creativity and its appeal to the surrounding region." The logo was chosen after some experimentation with slogans ("Little City, Big Taste") and was mocked up for demonstration on business cards, letterheads, pamphlets and, eventually, welcoming signs at the city's borders.

An effort to showcase the logo on city buses was short-lived. But in 2010, the design firm applied for trademark protection, and by 2014, Falls Churchians could order Virginia Little City vanity license plates.

Benton wrote in a December 2009 editorial: "'The Little City' is spot on. Kudos to Falls Church's own SmithGifford marketing firm for accepting the task, involving the entire community and delivering on a first-rate 'brand.'… This is exactly what marketing firms get paid the big bucks to do.…'Little' is, well, reality, and something considered a plus by many living here. Finally, 'City' is exactly what Falls Church is, technically as well as in spirit. It is not a 'village' or 'town,' but increasingly cosmopolitan, up-to-date and forward-looking."

5

LIFTING THE VEIL ON CITY GOVERNMENT

For decades, when 9,400 Falls Churchians sought to keep up with local government, they depended on spotty coverage in the *Washington Post*, *Washington Times* and the *Journal* newspapers. But the arrival of the *News-Press* in 1991 brought a new fixture at city council meetings. Editor-publisher Benton estimated he has attended, in person, at least 80 percent of the council's sessions over thirty-three years—often late at night. Suddenly, the squabbles over budgets, property taxes, development, management of city services and prickly politicians' personalities became accessible through the free weekly every Thursday. City staff found themselves coordinating—even taking advice—from this new avenue for information give and take.

Elections in Falls Church had been dominated since the 1950s by the volunteer candidate recruiting group Citizens for a Better City. A rival, more conservative group called the Falls Church Citizens Organization emerged in 1988 to offer alternatives, just as Benton was dipping a toe in city goings-on. Not wishing to lean toward one group, the fledgling *News-Press* invited both to the office and inaugurated a "Point-Counterpoint" pair of essays on its opinion pages. That allowed a revolving cast of spokespersons to have their say, while the paper's editorials were free to focus on issues and candidates rather than "parties."

The CBC, created in 1959 by such Falls Church activists as Louis Olom, Edith Abramson and Roger Wollenberg, focused on recruiting quality candidates for the jobs that, as of 2023, pay $9,200 a year. The networking group promoted high-quality schools and city services, development policies favoring business growth compatible with the city's neighborhoods

The Falls Church City Council chambers, which double as a courthouse, were rebuilt in 2018–19. *Gary Mester.*

and protection of the city's natural endowments and maintaining the city's independent status. The CBC doesn't take positions—that's left up to individuals. The FCCO, led by Stewart Edwards, Ned Studholme and others, started with informal circulated critiques of the current council, protesting "runaway taxes" and "threats" to the city's village character. Insurgents Cynthia Garner, Susanne Bachtel and James Slattery won seats in 1990 and attracted support from Mayor Dale Dover, Falls Church's first Black man to hold the job. Dover abandoned the CBC and sided with FCCO. But in 1992, CDC candidates Merni Fitzgerald, Jeffrey Tarbert and Robert Perry came roaring back, paving the way to elevate Vice Mayor Brian O'Connor to the position of mayor. Benton achieved success in satisfying both groups. FCCO member Anthony Meredith penned a letter for the March 25, 1993 issue, congratulating the *News-Press* on its third year. "The platform calls for a paper that is clean, fearless and fair. All three goals are consistently achieved," he wrote. "The publication of letters that criticize the *News-Press* adds credibility to the paper, and ultimately strengthens it. The *News-Press* courageously questions the one-party city council which prefers not to be questioned."

In April 1994, the *News-Press* hosted both groups in a two-hour roundtable in its office and published a transcript. An accompanying editorial noted that the CBC members "lean heavily on the importance of maintaining that they contend has brought good things to Falls Church. The other group challenges the quality of past CBC leadership and comes at the issues of governing more from the 'outside.'" Both groups took out advertisements.

In a "Point-Counterpoint" in the January 13, 1994 issue, the FCCO's Mary Slattery rebutted a charge that it is against business, pointing instead to the CBC's "undemocratic" nominating process. In a February 1994 essay, FCCO advocate Hugh Long hit the CBC for "endless growth of the city budget," which, he said, can't be blamed on population growth or inflation. "If Falls Church is to preserve itself, we must tie our expenditures to real increases in income." FCCO activist Jim Yarger, in the February 22, 1996 issue, complained that "Falls Church is highest taxed jurisdiction in the region." In that May's race, the CBC came up short, with independents picking up two seats and retiring Tarbert. The *News-Press* editorial titled "The Upset" called the CBC "listless" and looked forward to "fresh ideas."

Debate between the two groups became angry and ad hominem, as individuals were accused of "character assassination," and the need for a "muzzle" arose after the spread of "falsehoods." FCCO members, in

November 1995, were accused of leaking negative stories about the city government to local ABC news station WJLA, asserting improprieties in tax assessment, police leave and retirement practices. They denied the leak. But apologies were issued, and the aisle was crossed. In 1995, the CBC and "independents" came together on the need to beef up the funding of schools, which, for many, was the chief attraction of the Little City. "Most of us, whether FCCO or CBC, don't have the stomach for this type of politics," Mary Slattery wrote in a letter published on September 25, 1997. The FCCO's high-water mark came in the May 1998 elections. Four of its candidates triumphed, making this only the second time since 1959 the CBC didn't dominate.

Power seesawed between the two groups. The independents' agenda of reduced spending and quieter development was on the upswing. "The 1990s cast a pause over economic development," Councilman Phil Duncan recalled in 2022. "It was difficult to get anything out of the ground other than a Taco Bell."

But by 2000, the pendulum had swung back in the CBC's direction with the landslide elections of Robin Gardner, Ron Parsons and Lindy Hockenberry. "Lopsided Election Sweep; CBC Win Margin Largest Since '86," declared the May 4 headline. Defeated independent Sam Mabry said, "We're victims of success," attributing the change to Mayor Snyder and the "outstanding way he cleaned up all the major issues with his leadership the last two years." The *News-Press* editorialized that the "lack of any viable political alternative to the CBC is neither good for the city nor, for that matter, the CBC itself."

In 2003, the *News-Press* discontinued the "Point-Counterpoint" essays. In the month before the May 2004 elections, the CBC took the gloves off, blasting FCCO opponents who would "isolate Falls Church." "They have no plans for the future. They don't like overcrowded schools, but they ridicule those who work to build new ones. They ask a lot of questions, but provide no answers. They criticize those who participate in local government, but can point to no achievements of their own." In 2006, four CBC candidates faced no opposition.

In spring 1997, the Little City began buzzing that the popular community center—a "big box" built in 1968 alongside the government center and Cherry Hill—needed a rehab. The *News-Press* backed the spending and even recommended adding an indoor pool to the existing meeting rooms and basketball and ping-pong facilities. A *News-Press* editorial accused opponents of being NIMBYs ("not in my backyard"), because to renovate without expanding the center would hurt the "disenfranchised." Many in the FCCO

The weekly paper's earliest election coverage included a 1992 pivotal debate sponsored by the chamber of commerce, organized by Benton. *From the* News-Press.

thought the $2.5 million price was too high. Letters poured in with worries that a renovation would "destroy" Cherry Hill as an outdoor recreation site. Opponents proposed putting the project to a popular referendum that would force a "supermajority" vote of the council—since 1988 referenda were required only for projects representing 10 percent of the budget. The CBC countered, and Councilwoman Merni Fitzgerald led a drive to defeat the plan for a referendum. The *News-Press* agreed, and the pro-referendum campaign failed. On May 5, 1998, the council backed the spending.

The construction on the community center was completed in fifteen months, and the dedication was covered in the June 16, 2001 issue of the *News-Press*. In a coda in 2006, Benton complained after the city decided to raise revenues by charging non-city residents a fee to use the athletic facilities. Citing the resulting "empty" basketball courts and the benefits sports can bring to reducing youth delinquency and gang activity, Benton said the fees were "symptomatic of an us-versus-them" mentality toward the city's neighbors. The fees were discontinued.

Another controversy got a bit in the weeds. In late 1997, some on the city council became concerned with the approval process for new development. They readied nine changes to the city charter to propose to Richmond, among them moving zoning enforcement from the sometimes-powerful planning commission to the council itself, to streamline what many called a "Byzantine" bureaucracy faced by developers. They also gave the council more power to block projects. A December 25 story headlined "Loud Public Outcry Puts City Charter Changes on Hold" reported that former mayors and school board and planning chiefs had called for more explanation of such issues, including reducing the number of council members and electing the mayor directly. The dispute went on for years. A January 2001 letter from Edie Smolinski warned that the council was "Moving Too Fast with Charter Changes," and editorials warned against "one-party rule" work sessions out of public view. The proposed changes were trimmed.

A "charter change" ballot referendum was set for November 2002. In letters in the October 24, 2002 issue, four ex-mayors urged a "no" vote. The week before voting, a *News-Press* banner headline read, "Charter Change Referendum: Both Sides Claim Outcome Critical to City's Future." Benton's editorial recommended defeat, warning that Falls Church "will become persona non grata in eyes of the regional development community." The chamber display advertisement sent a similar message. But a counter-message sponsored by a coalition called Citizens for Charter Referendum argued that the changes "would protect schools from more overcrowding and stabilize homeowner taxes."

Election coverage in the November 7 issue of the *News-Press* told the tale: "63.2% Vote 'No' as High Turnout Crushes FC Charter Referendum. Observers of Both Sides Stunned." Benton's editorial called the vote "A Mandate to Push Ahead."

The two strains of Falls Church politics would continue to reveal themselves. One divisive question for the traditionally nonpartisan advocates was whether to pursue partisan endorsements. In March 2006, Michael Gardner assumed chairmanship of the Falls Church Democratic Party, and immediately, the local party broke a thirty-year practice and planned to endorse candidates for city council. Calling out the CBC for its "arrogance," independents such as Mabry decried the "ruling elite," prompting rebuttal letters from Bob Storck and Dick McCall, saying the CBC merely seeks "excellent candidates." A March 16 *News-Press* editorial decried "The Failure of the CBC" for denying that it was "time to move to another electoral model in FC." But the CBC attacked the plan because the partisan stamp would prevent federal employees from seeking office in Falls Church due to the federal Hatch Act that preserves a nonpartisan civil service. New leadership in 2008 prompted Democrats to cancel the endorsements.

The second dustup was triggered by a 2000 state law that permitted jurisdictions to move their local elections from May to November to increase participation on a day of higher voter turnout. As Benton wrote in 2011,

"The discussion began in the fall of 2009, when first-term Councilman Lawrence Webb raised the matter." "It seemed clear that voter turnout rates are significantly higher in November, when presidential and U.S. Senate races are on the ballot," he said. Opponents believed local elections should continue to be held in May, when budget discussions are fresh in voters' minds and local issues are less overshadowed by state and national politics. In 2011, the question was put to a referendum. Monitoring groups, such as the League of Women Voters and the Village Preservation and Improvement Society, were divided. The *News-Press* favored the change, but tempers flared and emotions ran high. Councilmen Dan Sze and Dan Maller took angry exception to Councilman Nader Baroukh's comment that even proposing the switch was "un-American." Councilman Webb rebuffed Councilman David Snyder's claim that ignoring 138 petition signatures favoring the May date amounted to "disenfranchising" citizens. Webb said that because he was a member of two minority groups (being Black and gay), disenfranchising anyone was furthest from his mind.

The decision to move elections to November passed in a 5–2 vote in May 2010 (then-mayor Robin Gardner, then-vice-mayor Hal Lippman, Sze, Maller and Webb voted "yes," while Baroukh and Snyder voted "no"). The U.S. Justice Department sanctioned the switch, which took effect in November 2013.

But there was collateral damage. In the May 2010 elections, CBC candidates were turned out (they had approved a $0.15 per $100 in assessed value rise in the property tax). The mini-slate of Johannah Barry and Ira Kaylin, both running for public office for the first time, finished solidly in all five Falls Church wards, while incumbent Snyder came in second overall, the *New-Press* reported. The result, after a national "Tea Party" election, was a more conservative fiscal policy. Even so, soon-to-be councilman Phil Duncan said moving to November elections was "the most important election in my time." "The following 2011 election was the dividing point between previous low-turnout election where assembling about 1,000 unhappy people was sufficient to win a council seat or two or three," he recalled in 2022. "After the move to November, the broader electorate proved to be progressive and less susceptible to single-issue groups unhappy over some particular economic development controversy."

The *News Press*'s efforts to stay neutral in editorials on elections were captured in Benton's May 2, 2002 essay titled "Well Informed & With Choice." It said "the city is far better served from feisty campaigns that command the public's attention." And there were occasions for skeptical commentary. "Council Cries 'Uncle!' Declares Utility Tax 'Dead on Arrival,'" shouted the April 11, 1991 banner headline after citizens spent four hours blasting a tax hike proposal. Benton's editorial support that year for entertaining a minor-league baseball team owner with the plan to bring a team to Falls Church (an estimated $5 million in new revenue) struck out. Though Benton drummed up enthusiasm with an essay contest on the love of baseball, the council, in September 1991, rejected the idea 4–3. In January 2007, he editorialized that "City Hall Still Doesn't Get It," blasting the failure to include a municipal parking garage in its five-year capital improvement plan to stimulate tourism.

In its three decades, the paper put out more general news and analysis of issues of the city council's handling of transportation, public safety, taxes, the pace of development, school budgets and parking wars. Its news items, editorials and letters gave readers the ins and outs of such issues as the council's April 2003 decision, after parental pressure, to require young people to show parental permission to check out sensitive library books. (Benton blasted it as "Stripping Budgets and Privacy Rights.") He applauded the council's 2003 resolution resisting the George W. Bush administration's

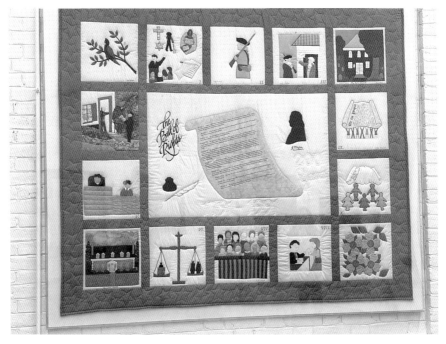

A citizen-made quilt celebrating the Bill of Rights was hung in the Falls Church City Council chambers in 1999, the city's tercentennial. *Author's photograph.*

alleged threat to domestic civil liberties under the Patriot Act, which was passed after the 9/11 attacks.

The *News-Press* gave mayors and city managers space in annual fully transcribed "State of the City" interviews. Officeholders tended to be cautious. Mayor Jeffrey Tarbert, in July 1994, said he was "Bullish on Falls Church." Mayor Dan Gardner, in August 2000, said his council was "a talented group" that "comes highly motivated." But Robin Gardner (no relation to Dan), the third woman mayor (following Betty Blystone and Carol DeLong in the 1980s), said in August 2008 that, despite a tightening of recession-era revenues from new mixed-use development, the city can avoid the shortfalls experienced by Fairfax.

City managers were treated as key personalities. In the paper's August 13, 1992 issue, the headline read "Doane Quits!" John Doane had been the city manager for only two years. Doane's reasons for leaving the position included that he wished "to be a private citizen," at a time of declining revenues, an eroding commercial base and split council decisions. In April 1997, the council was "Unanimous in Selection of Hector Rivera as New City Manager." By that November, the banner read: "Rivera Launches City Hall Shake-Up," a plan to shrink the number of departments from fourteen to five. "Falls Church is a small city," Rivera said. "It is a highly regulated environment. Much of the code is overly detailed, taking away from the discretion of the professional staff. As a result, an anti-business environment has developed."

By December, the *News-Press* had given Rivera's first six months "the highest mark," "exactly the tonic the City Council yearned for when it went hunting for a new city manager." But in June 1999, the banner read, "Rivera Resigns!" After an eventful two years, he was moving to Texas for family reasons. "Yes, he had a controversial style," read the editorial, but in Benton's own fourteen years in Falls Church, he'd "never seen more things happen to move the city forward than have occurred in the last two years." In January 2001, an anonymous letter accused independent councilwoman Kathie Winckler of racial prejudice for removing Hector Rivera as city manager and not hiring deputy Willie Best, a Black man, in his place. The council unanimously denounced the "smear," and a *News-Press* editorial said it was "Standing by Mrs. Winckler," printing her denial.

Steady stories of departures and deaths in city government became the paper's staple. The April 18, 1991 issue announced that School Superintendent Warren Pace would retire with four months' notice. In November 1995, City Attorney Peter Maier resigned to become assistant attorney for Arlington. The lead story for the February 12, 1998 issue was "City Half-Reeling from Resignation of CFO Doug Scott." In January 2003, Don Griner resigned from the planning commission after serving just weeks in a dispute over who would name the vice-president of the group. Such reporting highlights the value of an independent community newspaper, whose reporters dig deeper than simply reading a press release. The paper covered debates over the $13.5 million renovation of city hall (approved by a 5–2 council vote in December 2017). During the construction, from 2018 to 2019, the offices operated out of temporary space on North Washington Street.

Second only to the schools, the Mary Riley Styles Library is perhaps the top treasure of this small town where residents pitch in. Having opened as a regional pioneer in 1958, it was named, in 1977, for the Falls Church Women's Club's nineteenth-century library chairman who was raised across the street at the Cherry Hill farmhouse. A renovation that was started in 1992 prompted a *News-Press* headline in April 1993: "The Renovation of the Mary Riley Styles Library Is Complete and It's Beautiful." But by 2016 (in the digital era), the building was again in sore need of modernization and expansion. With a push from the library's foundation, funds were included in a ballot bond referendum of $8.7 million, which voters approved 2–1 that November. But the city council dillydallied, holding a town meeting. It wasn't until February 2020 (with the outbreak of a pandemic coming) that the council voted 5–2 to approve $11 million for the project, folding in $2.3 million from a general surplus. Construction was started by the Centennial Firm under a $7,866,308 contract, the *News-Press* reported, and the books and staff were moved temporarily to the Oak Street Elementary School. The shiny new library reopened in September 2021, the staff and most patrons wearing COVID masks.

A newspaper can deliver the human factor. Among the most abrupt and scoop-worthy developments in the city government's history was the July 2006 death of dynamic City Manager Dan McKeever (he passed away from melanoma at the age of fifty-seven). McKeever had come from Laconia, New Hampshire, in March 2000 to take what the *News-Press* called "a more aggressive approach to economic development." It would be "mixed use or nothing," he told city council in September 2002. McKeever had the delicate annual task of proposing "tight budgets" and balancing tax hikes with rising property assessments and the demands of school budgets. His authority grew when the Economic Development Administration was moved under his wing.

Giving lengthy interviews to the *News-Press*, McKeever also endured Benton's counseling on how to get messages to the public. "City Hall in a Struggle to Communicate," read the paper's headline on July 19, 2001. It seems players from the Washington Redskins were recruited for a summer youth reading session at the Falls Church library. But no youth showed up. "Communication is an important part of government," the paper said in an editorial. Benton said he wrote from experience, having been prompted to send multiple letters to six council members and accusing the city's Office of Communications of being *less* effective after expanding staff. McKeever subsequently tightened deadlines for departments to submit news items for the *Focus* newsletter (then produced with diskettes) and directed departments to issue their own press releases.

In 2004, McKeever had to deny a solid-sourced *Washington Post* story asserting there was a police quota for traffic tickets. And as the June 17, 2004 issue reported, it fell to him to apologize for the fire department after its crews arrived too late to rescue a cat named Tuffy from a storm drain.

After McKeever's death at the University of Virginia Hospital in Charlottesville was reported in the July 27, 2006 *News-Press*, the council named Assistant City Manager Wyatt Shields, then only thirty-seven, his successor.

The other sudden loss in the city government spotlight was the passing of two-term Councilman Dan Sze, who died in July 2020 after a bout with cancer at the age of sixty-nine. City Manager Shields announced Sze's death to the city staff. "All those who worked with him will miss his keen intelligence, his hearty greetings, and the jovial conversations they shared with Dan," Shields said. "Mr. Sze was a strong leader for environmental stewardship in his service on the city council and on regional and statewide policy boards. He strongly supported the new high school design for net zero carbon emissions." In July 2021, in a ceremony delayed by the pandemic, Sze was honored with the dedication of a plaque and gingko tree outside city hall.

6

Adventures in Development

T he core tension in Falls Church's land-use fracases pits the desire for revenue-enhancing development against the homey values of village-like streetscapes. As a roll call of controversies unfolded, individuals and political leaders—and the *News-Press*—won some and lost some.

In the paper's first year, the city council, after a year of hearings, approved probusiness zoning changes. As reported in the November 28, 1991 issue, the city imposed new requirements for street-level retail space for most development downtown, continued "by right" improvements by residential owners in transitional districts and prohibited freestanding multifamily uses in business districts. A breakthrough for the livability camp in 1992 was the opening of the $900,000 Citizens' Bridge, a two-span foot crossing over the traffic-filled Route 7. Its planning divided citizens. The feat was complicated by the fact that Falls Church owned the sidewalk, the road was owned by the Virginia Department of Transportation and the connecting Washington and Old Dominion Trail was owned by the Northern Virginia Regional Park Authority. But it's up.

In 1995, following what Benton called a "troubling" array of business closures, the city and the chamber of commerce launched a "public-private partnership" to coordinate with entrepreneurs, small businesses and investors. By 1997, it became, with *News-Press* encouragement, today's Economic Development Authority.

"Is Falls Church a City or Suburb?" asked Falls Church Citizens Organization member William Singletary in a commentary. The city

Controversial due to its multiple entities with jurisdiction, the Citizens Bridge, in 1992, raised a bike/pedestrian path over a traffic-filled Route 7. *From the* News-Press.

"solicits businesses to move here….It even holds 'economic summits,'" he said. Decades ago, it applied to the state to become a city. But "most of the time, the city seems to want to revert to its other status: a suburb, one with a top-notch school system and close to employment opportunities sustained by the federal government." Others warned of a "Tysonization" of the Falls Church "village," invoking a menace of Fairfax's Tysons Corner–style high-rises. In July 1993, the paper ran a photospread headlined "High Points at FC's First Economic Summit," at which eighty participants mapped out seventeen sites for development.

An early test of the new zoning came in 1993, when global PepsiCo Inc. announced plans for a drive-through Taco Bell on the lot of an abandoned gas station at the busy intersection of West Broad and West Streets. Neighbors considered the project tacky and warned it would attract traffic, late-night noise and crime while lowering nearby property values. The "Taco Wars" went on for weeks. An August letter from preservationist Louis Olom criticized the *News-Press* and business backers: "The indiscriminate development that you and your supporters advocate is no answer to the problems in Falls Church. For we are in no danger of financial collapse now or in the immediate future; nor have we been in the past." Council members

David Minton and Robert Perry were accused of having a conflict of interest by the newly formed the South West Home Owners Association. The two owned PepsiCo stock and had disclosed that fact when elected. Benton's editorial said, "Elected officials should not consider a majority but use their best judgment." The corporation made concessions on reduced hours and providing a security guard and outdoor trash receptacles. After the council gave its final approval in August 1993, the *News-Press* ran photographs of the construction, which bothered some who had opposed it. Benton's September 9 editorial praised both camps, lamenting "intemperate remarks" in a debate that pitted "revenues vs. quality of life."

"Pass the Hot Sauce," teased columnist Michael Hoover in the June 9, 1994 issue, alongside photographs of VIPs at the grand opening headlined "Big Enchiladas at Taco Bell." Once the Mexican fast-food joint was part of the landscape, reader Steve Williamson, in the February 16, 1995 issue, remarked on the "low incident level" of crimes and nuisances, praising "cooperative efforts" by all.

In October 1996, Mayor Jeff Tarbert announced at a chamber luncheon, "We are not a village. We live in urban America."

Across the border on the Fairfax County side on Hillwood Avenue stood the old Falls Church High School, opened in 1945. After its students moved to the new Falls Church High School on Jaguar Trail in 1967, the building was taken over by John G. Whittier Intermediate School. It closed in 1984. That old complex, by 1994, had become run-down and was being used as a food bank. But city managers, Mayor Brian O'Connor and builders were hungry for land, and after the building was declared unsafe, the city made a deal with Fairfax County to swap city-owned land at the west end, near George Mason High School, in return for Whittier's 9.6 acres on the city's east end. Fairfax got land for a planned graduate school center, while Falls Church got a doozy of a controversy.

Preservationists wanted to save the building as a piece of history. But as sentimental alumni gathered in March 1995 to witness demolition of their alma mater, economic consultants began envisioning: could Falls Church help fund its schools through commercial activity on the Whittier site? Or should it be sold to homebuilders for residential use that produces less revenue? Advocates for affordable housing asked the city to insist on enforcement. But letters to the editor, some from folks whom Benton called NIMBYs, resisted. "Slow Down on Whittier," the *News-Press* editorialized.

Benton recommended a public hearing. And by early 1997, the council was hearing "An Earful Against Whittier." Residents were skeptical there was commercial interest in developing the property; others warned against overcrowded schools. "Nimby Sentiment Rages Over ADUs at Whittier Site" said a story on the proposed eight affordable accessory dwelling units. One Benton editorial likened the issue to a horror film "that never seems to end." The CBC's Joe McDonald joked that "there hasn't been this much discussion since the Continental Congress."

But secretive negotiations began between O'Connor and Fairfax supervisor (and later congressman) Tom Davis. At the request of the Hillwood Association, it arranged traffic-calming measures along Hillwood Avenue, plus improvements to an athletic field. In 1997, the city sold the Whittier site to a residential developer for $9.6 million. After incalculable mental anguish, the net gain to the city was $8.26 million.

Meanwhile, as the Whittier deal emerged, the city was also bargaining with Fairfax over the price of 10 acres of west end land near the Metro stop slated for a graduate center for Virginia Tech and the University of Virginia. The city, years earlier, had bought a portion, the 7.42-acre Kiessling tract, for $283,000 and used the site near the high school for citizen garden plots. But Fairfax was eager to attract the universities, which is why it gave Falls Church a deal on Whittier. What resulted was neither a historical tribute nor affordable housing—it became the site of luxury townhomes.

The academic center regularly drew front-page *News-Press* coverage in 1994–96. "Grad Center Madness" it editorialized in February 1994, warning the city against "giving away its single most valuable asset for $1 a year plain and simple." Seen as a technology and economic incubator, the project also needed approval and state funding. But soon, the two universities demanded greater contributions from the city. "City Hit Up to Pay for Grad Center," read the headline in May 1994—UVA and Virginia Tech wanted $25,000 a year for twenty years. "No More Concessions," demanded an editorial. The planning commission and school board echoed that message. But in June, the city council coughed up more money.

In leasing the land, the city received $500,000 up front, with an agreement that the universities would foot the bill on a computer room and a distance-learning room at the high school next door for $400,000 and $35,000 a year for twenty years. The symbolic $1 a year for twenty years, it was calculated after later sales, actually gained the city $17.5 million.

News-Press "prescriptions" for development evolved, as Benton's editorial line conjured Falls Church becoming "an evening destination" like Alexandria's Old Town. The ingredients, an editorial in September 1996 said, are "already here" in the form of two Metro stops and an interstate

In 1997, after years of policymaker infighting over what to do with the former school property called Whittier, the city sold it to a homebuilder. *Author's photograph.*

highway (I-66) ready to "whisk families" into the nation's capital. "There is the safe, friendly, and attractive family environment we all treasure," he wrote. "But the first obvious missing component is sleeping space," meaning one or two larger hotels, recreational activities and shared swimming pools and parking. One naysayer was environmental consultant Dave Eckert, who wrote in a November 21, 1996 letter that the word "village has a soft sound," which is why people move here. Falls Churchians can "dream we're more like Bedford Falls than Pottersville," said the activist, who organized annual showings of the classic film *It's a Wonderful Life*.

That November's election brought the headline "All Incumbents Carry City," with an 86 percent turnout. The *News-Press* editorial interpreted the results as a "'Stay the Course' Mandate" for pursuing commercial development.

One shot in the economic arm was coming. The 1936 vintage movie house on North Washington Street, the State Theatre, had fallen on hard times due to competition from home video. It had stood empty since 1989, when Richmond authorities authorized its demolition. It was called "an eyesore, not deserving of the label 'historic,'" in an October 1996 letter written by William Jones.

But Virginia businessman Steve Cram bought the twelve-thousand-square-foot property from the movie chain. Preservation activist Carol Jackson and Delegate Bob Hull fished for angels to save it, even traveling to Richmond to study another old theater. "A State Theatre Rebirth?" asked the December 5, 1997 story on entrepreneurs Thomas Carter and David Steinberg. With city council encouragement, these men attracted investors for a $1.8 million renovation to the space that would include a multiuse restaurant, two bars and a conference center for private events. A *News-Press* editorial talked it up as an economic stimulus, recommending no parking requirements to ease the way. The planning commission delayed on the parking question. "A State Funeral?" asked the October 16, 1997 editorial. The delays continued into 1998, when, in August, entrepreneurs Carter and Steinberg asked the city for a $125,000 loan. "Loan 'Em the Money," the *News-Press* counseled.

In the end, with an $8,000 gift from the Village Preservation and Improvement Society, the State Theatre's restoration architect preserved the stage as a bandstand, kept the plush lobbies and vintage restrooms and moved two hundred of the original movie seats to the balcony for an overall capacity of 850. (They displayed objects from the demolition, including ancient packs of Jujubes and condoms.)

The first movie shown at the rehabbed State Theatre was Eckert's environmental documentary on Four Mile Run. "It filled the house, so we literally ran out of food," he recalled. But the official daylong ceremonial opening showcased the State Theatre as a concert venue, with the famed Cellar Door Productions booking the talent.

The May 20, 1999 *News-Press* talked of "A New Era in City," commenting, "The inside of the fully renovated building is breathtaking." The new destination—long lines appeared on weekend evenings on North Washington Street—tempted city hall to raise revenue through an "amusement tax," but that was defeated. In early 2002, after the chamber held a fête at the venue, the *News-Press* incorporated the State into its arguments for a "structured parking" facility. (The parking crunch was eased when Kaiser Permanente, across the street, allowed concertgoers evening parking for free.)

For much of the late 1990s, the *News-Press* boosted efforts to redevelop both eastward and westward of the Broad Street–Washington Street intersection. Benton proposed an artsy theater at the vacant Podolnick Property, named for Dr. Nelson Podolnick at 400 West Broad. A March 19, 1998 editorial expanded: "We've always advocated strongly for creative and aggressive…economic revitalization and development. However, we have always seen this not as an end in itself, but as a means for which our children can be assured of quality schools, and our seniors, our infirm and disadvantaged the services they require."

Consultant David Holmes was named to direct the Economic Development Authority, and he was called by the paper, on January 8, 1998, the author of the "Aggressive Community Scheme for City." A year later, the *News-Press* applauded the council's "sweeping" loosened zoning: "Unanimous Council Passes Sweeping New Mixed Use Law to Spark Economic Growth," read the story about MUR (Mixed-Use Redevelopment). On July 20, 2000, the council and the EDA, in a first, acted swiftly to buy the Podolnick property. In November 2001, the EDA assembled four development groups that liked prospects for "robust development." Soon, the city adopted a formal economic development policy stressing cooperation for competing in the regional and global economy.

Another step was a deal that was made between Falls Church and Arlington to upgrade their shared fire station on North Washington Street. "Council OKs Closing Deal on $6 Million New Fire Station," stated the July 30, 1998 headline. The city's share would be $3.637 million, and Arlington's would be $1.845 million (though Arlington would staff it). Falls Church's volunteer firefighters kicked in $464,380 for the new four-bay station at the "gateway to the city," designed by Dewberry Davis Design-Build. A *News-Press* editorial proclaimed the paper was "heartened by the Council's thorough discussion of cost." The paper published a photograph of the ground-breaking in August 1999, and in May 2022, it featured Quinn's Auction Galleries' efforts to raise money for the volunteer force.

One tempting distraction was the Technology Triangle, a vision of turning west end land at Route 7, around Gordon Road and Shreve Road, into a conference center for Northern Virginia's growing tech industry. The Beyer family of the Volvo dealership, which owned one-third of the land, announced the plan in September 1998. By July 1999, the headline read, "Beyer Says Tech Triangle Stalled Until City Commits Its Land." The project died a slow death. "David Holmes and the Tech Triangle are history," wrote city chief information officer Barbara Gordon in the July 21, 2001 issue. (Another false dawn came in November 2004, when a *News-Press* editorial counseled citizenry to "Look East." Just over the Arlington line at the East Falls Church Metro Station, the Arlington County Board, staff planners and neighborhood volunteers were envisioning Transit Town. They thought they could attract investors to include a new western entrance to the Metro on the Falls Church side, with the possibility of a minimart and café—even residential housing—on top. But a recession discouraged investment, and the plan remains on the drawing board.)

WHERE IS THE CENTER OF FALLS CHURCH?

But the city's landscape *was* changing. David Ross of Atlantic Realty signed a letter of intent to overhaul downtown blocks at Broad and Washington Streets around George Mason Square and over to Maple Avenue. Soon humming in the vicinity were Ireland's Four Provinces, the Pilin Thai Restaurant, Argia's Italian, the Broad Street Grill and the chain eatery Applebee's. Councilwoman Lindy Hockenberry and candidate Ron Parson urged the creation of a "town square." "City Gets a Downtown" became the *News-Press*'s top story in 2000, and Mayor David Snyder declared himself "pleased with the rapid rate at which developers are now beginning to step

The Harris Teeter mega-grocery and West Broad luxury apartments opened a new "city center" in July 2016. *Author's photograph.*

Top: Mason Square at Washington and Broad Streets is, to many, emblematic of the city. *Author's photograph.*

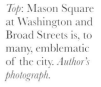

Middle: The Founders Row residential and restaurant complex, its name invoking George Washington and George Mason, opened in 2022 and moved the city's center west. *Author's photograph.*

Bottom: The stage at Cherry Hill Park is seen as the city's social center. *From the* News-Press.

forward and commit to major projects." In November 2001, the planning commission voted for mandatory design guidelines for buildings downtown. The agenda, at that time, was a "fundamental makeover of Falls Church," the paper editorialized.

In July 2001, the Dutch-based developer Waterford proposed replacing the vacant Adcom site (a former art supplies store at 500 West Broad Street) with the downtown area's first four-story, eighty-unit condo building, with some affordable housing units aimed at singles. It projected $220,000 in yearly revenue. "We like the idea of the kind of downtown 'The Broadway' will help Falls Church unfold," the *News-Press* editorialized. But in September, the headline read, "Planning Commission Dashes 'The Broadway,'" citing the health and safety impacts were not in conformity with the city's long-range plan. (Some neighbors were worried it would attract "the wrong element," and charges of discriminating against families with children were made.) But the final decision was the city council's: "The Broadway a Hit with City Council, Permission Granted." Construction began in April 2002. But FCCO critics, like Linda Neighborgall in her November 25, 2004 letter, said Benton's paper played a major role in creating a housing crisis by "incessant prodding, goading and promotion of high-density residential development on commercially zoned land."

The storm blew over. Waterford promise to donate five thousand tulips to the Broadway, and the George Mason High School chorus sang at the opening. "Development is on a roll in FC and there's no end in sight," the *News-Press* commented. "We Can Have It All," Benton editorialized in December 2004, "the best schools, the best neighborhoods, and the classiest commercial strip anywhere around."

Not all were enthused. There were fears of trampling on property rights. In a March 2004 letter to the *News-Press*, Ed Hillegass complained about a "great sucking noise" from big developers. "If the senior citizens don't wake up and smell the coffee in time, then most of us will have to sell our homes and leave this beautiful small-town city behind."

A block away from the Broadway, at 402 West Broad Street, a project by the Young Group was taking shape on the site of an auto repair shop. Bob Young's novel idea was to provide subsidized housing downtown on a "first dibs" basis to public school teachers. The Housing Corporation backed the plan to earmark twenty-six units for this purpose, and the newspaper, in September 2004, called it "A Bold First Step." The Historical Commission had been asked to suggest a meaningful name and came up with the Trammel, after a centuries-earlier landowner. But Trammel was likely an enslaver. So, Young, at Benton's prodding, named it instead for New England educator and abolitionist John Read, who is buried at Falls Church Episcopal. A ground-breaking for the Read building was held in June 2007.

Over the next decade, more mixed-use upscale structures appeared downtown. On the expanse of asphalt spread for the restaurant chain Red Lobster at 513 West Broad Street rose the condo development called the Byron. These ninety units, plus seven thousand square feet of retail (and restaurant) and office space and a parking garage, were built by developer Edward P. Novak Jr.

Waterford Development joined Akridge Real Estate Services to erect revenue-producing condos and a street-level retail project at 444 West Broad Street. Blueprints called for 191 condos, 32,000 square feet of retail and 29,800 square feet of office space. This was "The New Falls Church," enthused a Benton editorial. "The City has come of age with the project." It won approval with a divided planning commission and the council in March 2004. But a tall problem arose. A classic tree owned by nearby merchant Stephen Doudaklian of Bedo Leatherworks was to be preserved as a "matter of principle." After *News-Press* coverage, letters poured in favoring Bedo's position. Waterford, in May 2005, agreed to preserve the tree by digging underneath it, and the Spectrum opened in 2008.

On South Maple Street, a longtime duckpin bowling alley had fallen into disuse. (The empty building burned in May 2005.) The 4.7-acre Diener tract attracted a plan by Atlantic Realty for an office complex and condos (originally, the plan included some senior housing). But the housing component, with the fear of conversions to rentals (which would deny the city an estimated $185,000 in revenues), drew opposition. The final project was approved in December 2004. After the developers consulted with the Historical Commission, the project was called Pearson Square, after Simon Pearson, the colonial landowner. It became the site of condos and the Creative Cauldron Community Theater, and in 2007, the nonprofit publisher Tax Analysts moved in with two hundred employees.

On North Washington Street, near the Arlington border, developer Chris Bell of Hekemian & Co. set his sights on a 1920s funeral home called Pearsons. His proposal was to replace it with a four-story mixed-use residential building with 150 one-bedroom rental apartments. But neighbors at Jefferson and Columbus Streets showed up at council meetings to object, prompting a *News-Press* editorial "No Virtue in NIMBYism." Three years later, the March 2007 headline read, "Heikemian Finally

Wins OK for Northgate Project," with 105 renters, below-street parking and street-level merchants. Northgate opened in 2011 atop Café Kindred and a boxing gym. (As a proffer from the builder, a new historical plaque was attached streetside, describing the 1911 visit to the site by President William Howard Taft on his way to commemorate the fiftieth anniversary of the Battle of Bull Run.)

The development evolution was praised by Mayor Robin Gardner in an August 2007 interview: "We've brought in the Broadway, Byron, Spectrum, Pearson Square with the Tax Analysts building, Heikemian's project has been approved, and the Read is up. Prior to that, there'd been nothing for fifteen years."

Next came the Little City's quest for a city center. It would drift westward down Broad Street. (In April 2004, Representative Jim Moran helped secure a federal appropriation: "$2 million for engineering and construction costs of multi-use transit center downtown Falls Church.") The city adopted form-based zoning and raised allowable building heights to 85 feet or 115 feet if deemed "worthy" (the first such change in fifty-three years). As nearby Tysons Corner Mall opened a new wing, Benton warned that "Tysons is a harbinger of the massive new wave of development. Falls Church must position itself to become to Tysons Corner as Georgetown is to the District of Columbia."

"Ka-Boom! City Center Unveiled with a Bang!" shouted the December 14, 2006 headline, heralding the "1st Phase of New Falls Church." The paper published a rendering of a new hotel, grocery and residential complex at the "forgotten" 5.2-acre area from South Maple to West Broad Streets that could produce $2.8 million in annual revenues. It included an agreement that the Bowl America lanes on Maple Street would be moved across the street. Four firms bid. The planning commission, the chamber and the Village Preservation and Improvement Society backed the new city center. As City Manager Dan McKeever pulled levers, there was talk of using eminent domain.

But some were skeptical. An April 28, 2005 letter from Kathryn Kleiman disagreed with the *News-Press*'s pro-development editorial, arguing that "City Residents, Leaders Decide, Not Developers." The city's incorporation of a city center into its comprehensive plan scared small businesses that might be priced out. And the May 2006 elections gave the city council reason to hesitate. The *News-Press*'s voters guide noted that the city's property tax rate was just set at $1.01 for each $100 of assessed value. It was now the highest in the region. As impacts from the Great Recession hit, the council delayed and demanded more proffers from builders. Condo prices nosedived. "Developers Walk Away, Downsize Plans—Reacting to Market Stall and FC Rebuffs," the paper reported.

By the end of 2007, with a recession nigh, City Manager Shields killed the deal. So, a formal city center never materialized. But it arrived incrementally. The closest thing to it was the massive mixed-use project at 300 West Broad Street. It replaced the old post office (which was moved up the street) and Anthony's Restaurant (which was reopened on Annandale Road). This center was anchored by a major employer, the giant Harris Teeter chain grocery store (open twenty-four hours a day). Above it are the new apartments of WB, for West Broad, its grand opening held on July 21, 2016.

Spotting a need for more senior living facilities, the NoVa Ventures real estate firm bought the site of the Burger King at 700 West Broad Street. Offering an alternative to the Sunrise Senior Living on North Washington Street, it opened the Kensington on June 16, 2016. Another project aimed at that demographic was the Falls Church Railroad Cottages. The brainchild of Bob Young, the idea was to meet the demand for downsized home ownership by building with greater density. For a 1.25-acre site off West Broad Street, the blueprints in September 2017 sketched ten cottage units, each comprising 1,500 square feet, with one and a half stories and a common house, designated for ages fifty-five and up and no one under eighteen. The plan had been supported by most boards and commissions. Its promise as a sustainable development encouraged Northern Virginia Parks to permit an easement to widen Railroad Avenue from eight to sixteen feet.

Neighbors in single-family homes alongside the site were not thrilled. Letters to the *News-Press* warned of poor access for fire engines. "There are

The award-winning Railroad Cottages, built densely and reserved for seniors, were controversial among neighbors in 2017. *The Young Group.*

other short-term issues, like noise, light and air pollution from the proposed parking lot impacting the neighbors, parking and safety, which also need to be addressed," wrote David Jacobs in an August 24, 2017 letter. But the council voted to grant the necessary easements, and Young agreed to contribute to the City's Affordable Housing Fund. Construction was completed, units were sold, residents moved in and the project received national attention as a trailblazer in tasteful density. In October 2020, the American Planning Association gave the Railroad Cottage Project the Red Clay Award for Development of the Year.

One controversy favored the forces prioritizing sustainability and preservation. The Fellows Property at 604 South Oak Street, adjacent to Jefferson Elementary School, was long the home of the Fellows family—Harry Fellows, in the 1920s, was mayor. Betty Fellows, an occupant of the vintage home on 1.8 acres in the Virginia Forest neighborhood, had lived her entire life on the site. Her will left the tract to the Fellows Living Trust, her family. At the time of her death, in September 2017, the trust had just won the planning commission's preliminary approval to subdivide the property into seven parcels for residential development. Fellows had been adamant about not selling her land to the city.

But city officials, years earlier, had discussed retaining the right to condemn or invoke eminent domain on her land for government purpose. "How Dare the City!" shouted a June 30, 2016 letter to the editor from Kathleen Luisa. "What a bunch of pathetic vultures! To lie in wait to snatch what belongs to other people through any means is reprehensible. In justice the properties of every Council member who agrees with this ought to be taken the same way."

In December 2018, the council, by a 6–1 vote, authorized City Manager Shields to pursue acquisition for "parks or school." The leafy Fellows tract was incorporated into the city's master plan to provide an open space or a school. Historian Bradley Gernand helped explain the benefits of the site's original state, and plans for school improvements were directed elsewhere. The community was further divided. Next-door neighbor John Transue, in a December 2018 letter to the editor, argued that "taking personal property is a serious action…justified only if necessary." "The city has not revealed a plan," he added. He suggested officials were seeking to degrade the land's value below market value to make it easier to acquire.

But the city's new capital improvement plan earmarked the land as a park. A city survey of four hundred showed a preference for "passive recreation, like walking and wildlife observation." In February 2019, the city finalized the purchase for $4,667,110. In May 2020, the home was torn down, and the resulting park is now widely visited.

The *News-Press* has been only mildly supportive of historic preservation. In spring 1996, a developer planned to build townhouses at 200 East Broad Street, the site of an 1890 home called the Proctor house. Preservationists with Historic Falls Church Inc., along with Keith Thurston of the Village Preservation and Improvement Society, proposed moving the former boardinghouse and doctor's office east to 303 East Broad Street on land next to the park named for the late Falls Church Public Works director Donald Frady.

The paper's May 30 guest commentary backed the plan, but neighbors Alan and Margaret Rudd complained about the change to their block, a private residence in a public park. The Proctor move subsequently drew support in a September 1996 letter from Councilman David Snyder, who noted that, while the project required a change in the master plan, the relocated house would help attract tourist dollars and was backed by the city's public-private partnership, the business development commission and the advisory board on recreation and parks. In mid-December, Broad Street

City father Don Frady, a longtime director of public works, visits the park named for him shortly before his death in 1994. *From the* News-Press.

In 1996, the aging Proctor house, a former doctor's office and boardinghouse, was moved by preservationists from downtown to an East Broad Street park. *Author's photograph.*

was closed, and the entire structure was moved at a cost of $150,000. A letter from Madge Creasy in April 1997 congratulated the city on preserving that "creaky, shaky old house."

The developer community's bugaboo known as affordable housing, by contrast, was steadily talked up by Benton. He decried NIMBY resistance to projects for seniors or low-income residents. "Stiffing Affordable Housing," read his June 10, 2004 editorial after a fifty-six-unit senior housing project near a park at 900 West Broad Street was fought over. "The council left its creativity hats at home." An opposing letter from John Murphy in the May 12, 2005 edition blasted the *News-Press* for its stance pushing multifamily housing, saying, "The exclusionary zoning for townhouses and multi-housing was enacted 25 years ago to protect the character of the city."

Carol Jackson, the head of the Falls Church Housing Corporation, worked (unsuccessfully) to put affordable housing units on Annandale Road near Maple Avenue. "The city council was sensitive about offending the sensibility of towns people who moved there in the 1980s and '90s for education and affordability," she recalled in 2022. "They basically wanted to close the gates. I became known for beating my head against every brick wall in Falls Church as the NIMBY attitude of 'just not here' won repeatedly."

The *News-Press*'s editorial "The Assessor's Message," in January 2003, challenged the "trickle down" argument that luxury housing creates opportunities for moderately priced housing. A December 2004 story on a city housing division report said only 6 percent of the Falls Church population can afford to buy.

"Affordable Housing Needs Intentional Effort," Jackson wrote in a June 16, 2005 letter to the editor. The project she championed was a proposal to use city land on the west end for affordable housing in five-story, twenty-nine-thousand-square-foot structure. But the goal clashed with neighbors' desire for park space, and hoped-for grants from the federal and state governments fell through. "A Penny for FC's Future" read the *News-Press* editorial for April 16, 2006.

The planned unit for seniors on South Maple Avenue gained momentum in 2008, even as the country entered a recession. "The Housing Corp. had pulled a rabbit out of a hat," resurrecting a failed project at the Atlantic

The condos/apartments centrally located on West Broad Street and Virginia Avenue include both market-rate and subsidized rental spaces. *Author's photograph.*

Realty office building, Jackson recalled. Though Benton's use of the term *NIMBY* was not always helpful, "he was instrumental in keeping people's feet to the fire." Federal stimulus funds arrived in 2009, and the project was "shovel-ready." But when conservatives won the council in May 2010, they voted to deny the contract. "We had to close the Falls Church Housing Corporation" by merging with the New York–based NHP Foundation.

Flash forward to September 2022: the *News-Press* reported "Major Affordable Housing Deal Set." The council voted 7–0 for a memorandum of understanding to transfer ownership of five four-plexes in Virginia Village on South Maple Avenue from the city to the Wesley Housing Development Corporation of Northern Virginia.

To keep tabs on the private sector, the *News-Press* relayed business publication stories' updating developments—the 2000 arrival of a Starbucks at the Broaddale Village Shopping Center, for example, and awards to the Kastle Systems building security firm. In August 2018, the council, following a six-year process, approved plans for Founders Row (an allusion to George Washington and George Mason). It involved a complex of 322 luxury apartments, plus 72 senior and affordable units. The site at West and West Broad Streets required buying out longtime merchants Shreve McGonigle Plumbing Supplies, Action Music, the Lazy Sundae Snack Shop, a 7-11 and Ken Currle's Sunoco Station that had been on the site twenty-five years. Founders Row now hosts restaurants Ellie Bird, Chasin' Tails and Nue. With construction mostly completed in 2023, the developer Mill Creek Residential Trust added the icing on the cake— thanks to advocacy by the *News-Press*—a seven-screen, post-pandemic IMAX movie theater seating six hundred.

That announcement was followed in the winter of 2022 by Insight Properties' development at the central intersection at Broad and Washington Streets. This meant demolishing the jewelry and computer stores and the Applebee's chain restaurant to make room for a mega–Whole Foods Market, the Creative Cauldron Community Theater and affordable housing. In the city's single-largest development—the result of the city's deal with Fairfax County to trade its water system for land—Hoffman and Associates, in August 2022, supplied details on its planned ten-acre, transit-oriented, mixed-use project in Falls Church's west end. That "gateway to Falls Church" will include condos, apartments, senior living spaces, retail spaces, a hotel, a medical building and eighteen thousand square feet for a community gathering place. "[It is] the biggest project in Falls Church history," said the press release. The Trammell Crow Company won city council approval in

The city's largest project ever was underway in 2022–23. It includes condos, apartments, senior living space, retail space, a hotel and a medical building on the city's gateway from Fairfax County. *Author's photograph.*

October 2022 to build a senior housing project on the west end (though the Texas corporation later backed out). That future project could include the city's tallest building—fifteen stories.

The blitz of activity is a far cry from the days of warring over Taco Bell.

7

SCHOOLS

The Key Ingredient

Why do most people move to Falls Church? Why stretch one's budgets for high mortgage payments and advocate (sometimes) for raising one's property tax? Often, it's to boost a key ingredient to the Little City's appeal: its admired public schools. The *News-Press*'s push for revenue-enhancing commercial development was always linked to maintaining the schools, which also form an essential ingredient to the paper's contents.

The five schools that today serve 2,600 students (and include a K-12 International Baccalaureate Continuum) formed the chief reason for Falls Church's incorporation as an independent city in 1948—or so it is argued. Beginning in February 1997, a debate broke out in the newspaper's pages. NPR reporter Peter Overby, whose parents had worked for the city's independence in the 1940s, asserted in a commentary that schools were the chief reason. But in August 1998, at a forum marking the city's fiftieth anniversary, the headline read, "New Research on Falls Church's Move to Independent City Status Shows Schools Were Not the Prime Motive." Resident Shirley Camp, citing original documents, argued that the main reason Falls Church wanted recognition as a city from Richmond was a fear of being overshadowed by Arlington. A subsequent letter from Jane Dexter cited a 1951 *Washington Post* piece headlined, "Schools Are Focus of Falls Church Ballot Battle."

The *News-Press* sided with Overby. "Yes, it's true, Virginia," ran the September 3 editorial, "that people are willing to cram their families into small townhouses in order to be within our city limits and have their children attend our schools." Schools are "Falls Church's principal industry." One booster of independence had been Jessie Thackrey, a school board member who died at the age of one hundred in 2013 and for whom the public preschool on Cherry Street is named.

Some coverage flattered readers. "Falls Church has the second highest percentage of adults with college or secondary degrees in United States," noted an editorial from November 23, 1995. The banner headline for the August 29, 1996 front page read, "Falls Church School SAT Average Ranks Tops in Metro Region Again." And on May 17, 2001, the *News-Press* reported that George Mason High School (since renamed Meridian High School), for the fourth year in a row had been ranked number 1 among 145 Washington-area high schools in the "Challenge Index," compiled by *Newsweek* based on enrollments in Advanced Placement classes. "Hats Off to the Schools," the editorial applauded. On February 5, 1998, the paper ran a photograph of the high school's District Academic Champions. And Mike Hoover wrote a column in January 1998 on the *Washington Post*'s Jay Mathews's description of George Mason High School as "the most challenging high school program in the country."

Editor Benton, early on, made inroads in the high school, running an eight-photograph spread in the October 1, 1992 issue titled "A Day in the Life at GMHS." He executed a feature on the bullying of kids with disabilities for the February 4, 1993 issue titled "The Inclusion Project: The Politics of Caring in the School Yard."

Soon, the school PTSA and student associations were taking out advertisements and republishing their newsletter the *Maverick* in the *News-Press*. The high school band performed at *News-Press* holiday parties, and the paper regularly sponsored a "Day at the Ball Park" on campus. The high school's small size (graduating classes usually number between 100 and 200) made the coverage intimate: sports, keepsake color photographs of the entire senior class at graduation (on the outdoor bleachers or on the basketball court), upbeat reports on the all-night (alcohol-free) "enchanted evening" graduation celebrations ("They All Clean Up So Nicely," read the headline for the May 2004 bash at the State Theatre) and New Year's parties, prestigious graduation speakers, front-page photographs of high school theater productions from *Guys and Dolls* and *Harvey* to *Ten Little Indians*, college scholarship recipients (whom Benton helps fund), full lists of the graduates' plans for college or employment and even private parties and features on alumni who return to share proud tales.

The paper covered the October 2002 tragedy in which two alumnae from the class of '02 died in a car accident near Emporia, Virginia. And in 1998,

Student thespians at Meridian High School trumpet the local paper in their November 2022 production of *Pippin*. *From the* News-Press.

it ran a photograph of George Mason students posing with a wrecked car as a "sober reminder" against drunk driving.

For the lower grades, the paper published smiling photographs of the Mount Daniel preschoolers' *Happy Hippo Show* and the Thomas Jefferson Elementary Sock Hop, drawing thankful letters from parent organizers.

A letter in the July 1, 1993 issue from high school PTSA president Mike Mohajeri said, "I believe that the comprehensive coverage of the school events by the *News-Press* has been a great boost to our school and community spirit." In July 1999, 1,200 Falls Church City Public Schools alumni returned for a picnic at Cherry Hill to celebrate the system's fiftieth anniversary. It featured one hundred teachers and former superintendents in a panel discussion. The May 5, 2005 issue reported on Timber Lane Elementary's celebration of its fiftieth year nearby in Fairfax County. Later that year, the paper branched out to report on a similar event at nearby McLean High School.

But it was not all boosterism and fun. In early 1992, controversy broke out when the student newspaper the *Lasso* published sensitive articles debating whether "AIDS Results from Making a Choice" versus "AIDS Can Happen to Anyone." This led the school paper to publish two advertisements from gay advocacy groups, the Area Clinic Defense Task Force and the Sexual Minority Youth Assistance League. A *News-Press* editorial praised the students for their bravery but worried that they "clouded the issue" of how adolescent sexuality should be discussed. Similarly, in March 2003, the *News-Press* gave approving coverage of the *Lasso*'s candid reporting on the extent of student substance abuse.

Still, the bulk of *News-Press* coverage would tackle the annual city council and school board budget dramas, the comings and goings of school officials (some involuntary), the battles over expanding school facilities and the delicate questions surrounding the names of schools.

It was in April 1994 that conservative and liberal factions on the city council united in agreement for the full funding of schools. A year later came the lead story that the chamber of commerce "Backs Full Funding of School Budget." The *News-Press* editorial cheered "Hurrah for the Chamber." That meant the school board gave approval to restore the cuts requested that year by Superintendent Stewart Roberson.

In most cycles, there was tension. In April 1998, for example, City Manager Hector Rivera submitted a budget that would have trimmed the schools' request by $359,000, prompting school leaders to resist his claims of no harm. "Council Gets Earful from Public Supporting School Budget," stated the headline above a photograph of protesting parents with copies of the *News-Press* over the heads. An editorial warned of "The Impending Talent Drain" if teachers' pay wasn't raised. It was up to the council. The April 23 headline read, "Council Has Will, Finds Way: School Board Budget OK'd With No Tax Hike." Thanks to a newfound $218,000 windfall, the editorial was titled "A Sigh of Relief," and the editor added his name to a list published in an advertisement: "We support our schools and are willing to pay for it."

By 1999, the challenges had heightened. "Enrollment Growth Drives Superintendent Recommendation for 10.45% School Budget Hike," read the January 14 banner headline. Mayor Snyder said he would not support the hike. Negotiations between the council and school board lasted until April, when the headline read, "New Budget to Fully Fund Schools and Provide Decades First Tax Cut." The editorial heralded "A Bright Future" in the city's "new-found prosperity bubble not likely to burst anytime soon."

But Superintendent Mary Ellen Shaw wasn't done. In January 2000, she proposed a 9.6 percent increase to accommodate an 8.7 percent enrollment rise in a $17.5 million budget. This came when real estate assessments had risen by 7.25 percent, and school construction costs were up. "The High

Price of Success," read the editorial. "We cannot avoid these costs without threatening a serious decline in the quality of our schools and our lives." By February, the school board was asking for only a 3.6 percent hike, and by March, the city manager submitted a "Budget With No Tax Hike and Full School Funding."

The *News-Press* was launched just as School Superintendent Warren Pace was ending his admired tenure (1971–91). Voters that year approved a $12.8 million bond referendum to expand and renovate both George Mason High School and the city's middle school. "Landslide!" exclaimed the June 6, 1991 report that 62 percent of voters had backed the first improvements to those school buildings since the early 1950s. The largest construction project in city history, including the completion of new labs, a gym and auditorium, was celebrated in May 1995.

The newspaper reported on leaders' arrivals and departures through the current (2023) superintendent, Peter Noonan. In August 1991, it wrote up the arrival of Stewart Roberson, fresh from Fredericksburg, Virginia, and later his departure for Hanover County in May 1994. In January 1993, the *News-Press* broke the story that school board member Kay Wilson was quitting, disgruntled by the system's decision to suspend rather than expel a seventh grader who'd come to school with a BB gun.

Public school officials, in April 2004, enjoyed the rare groundbreaking for a new building called Mary Ellen Henderson Middle School. *From the* News-Press.

In October 1994, the school board tapped Patricia Dignan of Ypsilanti, Michigan, for the top job. But just over a year after her arrival, the paper ran a December 1996 exclusive: "School Board Negotiating Early Termination of Dignan Contract." In January, it was revealed that the system had to pay a remaining $300,000 on her four-year contract. She wrote to the *News-Press* accusing the school board of "cronyism" before resigning with a $140,000 payment. A February 1997 rebuttal from Paul Ferentinos of the Falls Church Education Association said Dignan didn't confer on the budget with the Professional Employees Advisory Committee. In an editorial, Benton wrote that he was "sad" Dignan was leaving but noted that the decision was up to the elected board and that he wasn't "privy to their inner workings." No stories against her were "planted" by the board, he added. Dignan, in a final letter in March, called the accusations "half-truths," and she said she "hopes this ends the board's efforts to discredit me."

The system's successor fared better. Mary Ellen Shaw was a three-decade veteran of the Falls Church system. Sworn in in 1998, she began dealing with rising enrollment that required trailers on campus. She took the schools through the trauma of the 9/11 terrorist attacks in 2001, praising staff for their response. She installed a phone in every classroom for safety and spoke at the Fall Festival that assembled representatives of Muslim, Jewish, Christian, Sikh and Baha'i faiths for unity. In May 2004, a soon-to-retire Shaw was the grand marshal of the Memorial Day parade, and a tree was planted for her at Mount Daniel Elementary.

The school system's lurching efforts to expand its facilities on limited land produced much drama—and copy for the *News-Press*—combining, as such fights do, the politics of budgets, development and neighborhood resistance. One example was the August 1998 request from the schools to have city council spend $1.7 million to modernize the athletic fields around the high school and middle school. It was approved a month later, but Falls Church Citizens Organization member Linda Neighborgall mocked it as a "field of dreams." Benton donated money for a new scoreboard that would display the *News-Press* logo. By August 2000, the twelve-acre site, with seats for 1,975, was ready for the high school football opener. It was officially dedicated that November by retired football coach Jack Gambill.

But not all functioned well. In May 2002, a high school baseball game was called off due to a "design flaw in the renovated athletic fields," the paper reported. The flaw "permitted fly balls to fly onto access road at I-66," and school board chair Jay Grusin explained that architects had miscalculated fence heights. The problem was solved with a net to catch balls.

More ambitiously, in November 2001, the headline read that the superintendent "Unveils Plan to Build New Elementary School for $13 Million." Rising enrollment had forced some teachers to shift classrooms and push supply carts. At this point, there was no land available for a third elementary school, even if it would require no sports fields. By November, an announcement came that Madison Park, in a residential area off North Washington Street, behind the Sunrise Retirement Community, would be home to a new $16 million school. The drawing board concept of four hundred students in twenty-one classrooms by 2005 was backed by a *News-Press* editorial. It was a "cause for celebration, our first new school in 50 years," wrote board chair Gruisin, and it was backed by Mayor Dan Gardner.

But letters to the editor revealed nearby residents were protective of the existing park. "As Cat Stevens asked, 'Where will the children play?'" wrote Barbara Mahony in January 2003. Gerard Mene argued that "Madison Park is a city park," so weren't there alternative sites? The *News-Press* discovered that other sites had been scouted by developers, among them the Diener property (site of the South Maple Street duckpin bowling alley), a slice of the new Graduate Center on the west end and even the historic Cherry Hill. In the end, the decision was made to let Madison Park be and—working with Fairfax County, which owns the land—a wing with four classrooms would be added to Mount Daniel Elementary.

Attention that year shifted to plans for a new middle school building, a more ambitious project that was put to a public referendum in November 2003. An alliance of developers had already been selected and, in a first, was given direct control to accelerate the process. "77% say 'yes' to Funding New School," stated the *News-Press*. After an astonishingly short two years (under the Fairfax County permitting process), construction was completed alongside the existing building.

Along the way came the delicate question of renaming George Mason Middle School, the name considered redundant with George Mason High School. By December 2004, the suggestions were boiled down to keeping George Mason or switching to the name of his wife, Ann Mason; Eleanor Roosevelt; Dolley Madison; or Tripps Run (a nearby stream). But the banner headline in the January 27, 2005 *News-Press* read: "New Middle School Named for Legendary African American Educator Mary Ellen Henderson." The editorial hailed it as a "magnificent, earth-shaking paradigm-altering move." That September, the headline read, "Mary Ellen Henderson Middle School Dedicated on Namesake's 120th Birthday." The ceremony was attended by civil rights activist Edwin Henderson II, her grandson, along with some of her former students.

The removal of the Mason name was a harbinger. Over the next fifteen years, as the nation underwent a reinterpretation of the Founding Fathers' role in slavery, momentum built for changing the names of both George Mason High School and the city's Thomas Jefferson Elementary School. Beginning in June 2020, the school board solicited suggestions from hundreds of citizens, including staff and alumni. No fewer than thirteen public meetings were held, along with presentations to the board. Letters to the *News-Press* tended to favor name changes, citing the negative impact of slaveowners' names on minority students. On December 8, 2020, the board voted unanimously to change both schools' names. Superintendent Noonan formed two advisory study committees to recommend five names for each school. George Mason alumna Judy Fischer White wrote a letter proposing Horizon High, Virginia High, Academic High, University High and Providence High.

In its April 27, 2021 issue, the *News-Press* reported that the board had unanimously selected the name Oak Street Elementary for the Jefferson School, because "it is the school's original name, evokes a sense of place, and recognizes how trees are essential natural elements of Falls Church." And with a vote of 5–2, the board decided to replace George Mason's name with Meridian, based on the original 1791 meridian helping delineate the borders of Washington, D.C. (plus it's a direct nod to the school's history of educating global citizens through the International Baccalaureate Programme). The changes took effect that July.

Public schools, of course, needn't depend completely on taxpayer largesse to seek excellence. In December 2003, a group of community activists, including Dick McCall, Kieran Sharpe and Bob Young, supported by Nick Benton, put the finishing touches on the creation of a 501(c)(3) nonprofit called the Falls Church Education Foundation. Its mission: ensuring the equity of access, staff readiness and student preparedness for the twenty-first century. In April 2004, the group successfully petitioned the city council for $50,000 in seed money. Today, the foundation is staffed by two part-time employees, raising funds through donations, an annual distance race, a golf tournament and a gala-auction. In 2016, it expanded to administer the Samuel J. Waters Fund for the Arts, named for a Mason High School alumnus and singer who died of cancer at the age of twenty-two.

Several *News-Press* stories demonstrated that public schools need not be bureaucratically hidebound. In March 2003, the school board agreed to change in its policy of paying tuition for qualified Falls Church residents who win acceptance at Fairfax County's elite Thomas Jefferson High School for Science and Technology. The Fairfax authorities had demanded the contributions, but some in Falls Church felt it was an option that wasn't their duty to encourage. Within a week, after fielding discussions about the worthy goal of supporting high-achieving youth, the board reversed itself and continued providing the subsidy.

A more personal case arose in 1996. Student Marta Eckert, who was being homeschooled by her parents, wanted to play in the George Mason High School band. In August that year, the school board voted 4–2 to reject the request, on the basis that public school extracurriculars are for public school students. That logic was condemned in letters and a *News-Press* editorial, noting that the system was already allowing twelve tuition-paying students from outside schools to play. The student's father, Dave Eckert, recalled in a 2022 interview how much Benton's support touched him. "Schools in Falls Church are apple pie, right or wrong. We weren't opposed to the schools," he said, describing himself and his wife as leftist homeschoolers in a movement often associated with right-wingers. "But Nick really backed Marta in concept and put himself in an awkward position." Marta was allowed to join the band.

The paper did not neglect parochial and private schools. St. James Catholic, founded in 1947, appeared in the paper for its fundraisers and building improvement—and for being named, in June 1999, one of the 266 U.S. Blue Ribbon Schools. Two years earlier, the paper reported that the school's principal of twenty-five years, Sister Janet (Regina Dougherty), had won "Principal of the Year" for the Atlantic states. When the school's new Knecht Gym was dedicated in January 1999, the paper covered the ceremony, which was attended by hundreds. In June 2004, the paper covered the big day for forty-one new graduates of the Pimmit Hills Alternative High School. And in 2005, reporter Darien Bates wrote a feature on the Spring Street Daycare and Preschool that was founded in 1957 by the Sisters of the Missionary Servants of St. Joseph under the Columbian Province.

As the *News-Press*'s reach grew, it covered Falls Church High School (in Fairfax), as well as nearby McLean and Marshall High Schools. In June 2007, Benton was taken to task by a reader for his commentary on Hollywood actor Ben Affleck's graduation speech at Falls Church High. Jo Acosta accused the *News-Press* of bias toward the downtown high school. Benton wrote a brief apology, saying he was attempting to comment on "celebrity culture," not to disparage Affleck.

One area in which the heroics of the Falls Church City Public Schools were detailed was in its handling of the pandemic. "COVID-19 Positivity Rates Still High as F.C. Classes Resume," read the headline for September 10, 2021. "With the Falls Church public school year a week in, classes continue to be 100 percent in person at all grade levels and there are no missing students from the year of virtual learning," Benton wrote on page 1. "However, this is in the context of rates of transmission of the COVID-19 virus that are 'high' in the judgment of the Virginia Department of Health, and officials are continuing to watch very closely to determine that the current in-person environments are not triggering major new outbreaks." The schools were enforcing policies of indoor masking (with medical exemptions) and health aides testing students who feel ill, sending some home as necessary. "No one will be allowed to return to in-person learning until contact tracing is complete."

It was a prime example of *News-Press* "news you can use."

8

A Community of Worship

A ny American village or suburb with *church* in its name is bound to host houses of worship. And as a modern community newspaper, the *News-Press* devoted sympathetic ink in ways that would distinguish the paper from local predecessors by broadening coverage to reflect the religious diversity of a changing America.

Yet the famous namesake institution—the Falls Church Episcopal, which has been active since eighteenth-century colonists drew maps of the region— would receive the steadiest attention. Its treatment by the editor struck some readers as aggressive. But the paper's exclusives drew global notice. Early coverage was routinely positive. A March 11, 1993 item showcased the delivery of a "2,671 Pipe Organ," manufactured by Steiner-Reck, to the church. A feature in February 1998 heralded the eight-hundred-pound bronze bell that was made in Baltimore in 1895 and given to Falls Church Episcopal by Caroline Bell McGuigan and her husband.

The first hint the *News-Press* would report skeptically on Falls Church Episcopal emerged in June 2000, when the vestry announced that as a property owner for centuries, the church was proposing to close a city street. A photographic rendering by the church's attorney showed how East Fairfax Drive would be made private for the construction of an $18 million "parish life" education center, along with a fellowship hall and gym, to accommodate a congregation that had grown to 2,200. The problem? The street contained the Southgate Shopping Center, home to restaurants, a bookstore, a baker and a school uniform shop, alongside the Merrill House high-rise apartment complex and some condos. That seventy-four-thousand-square-foot shopping strip would have to be demolished. Donations for the construction from parishioners poured in, gifts some would regret. The expansion of the nonprofit church's holdings would deprive the city of $200,000 in annual tax revenue. A petition in opposition raised concerns about traffic, parking and utilities. The *News-Press* asked, "What's Love Got to Do With It?" It editorialized against the expansion, saying it "would significantly disenfranchise" 160 families in Merrill House. "Unfortunately, simply calling oneself a church has little to do in our society with being necessarily, morally, spiritually, authentic."

Church activists rebutted. A September 2000 "Viewpoint," written by Reverend John Yates, defended the purchase as a way to "reclaim history" from the nineteenth century, which "brought it back home" for such activities as kindergarten classes and Alcoholics Anonymous meetings.

On page 1 of the paper's June 7, 2001 issue, Benton wrote a news story under the headline "Church Draws Regional Spotlight by Cutting 'Simon Legree' Image in Evicting Restaurant," a reference to the cruel slave overseer

Historic Falls Church Episcopal drew mixed coverage for its ill-fated plan to close a street and when a divided congregation had a legal battle over the ownership of the land. *Author's collection.*

in *Uncle Tom's Cabin.* The church was evicting the Kurdish Ceilov Restaurant, run by Ali Shali, and news cameras were on the scene for what Benton described as the church absorbing "only the latest in public relations blows." Reverend Yates countered, saying the church "has been charitable, more than gracious.…The eviction has nothing to do with the church's future plans for construction on the Southgate property but instead results from Mr. Shali's nonpayment of rent."

In the end, the church canceled its plans for closing off the street but expanded its facilities on campus, though some donors demanded their money back. "Church Abandons Bid to Close Off Downtown Street," came the news in May 2002. Attorney Bill Baskin said, "We've determined that the Falls Church City Council would prefer not to see the street closed."

The *News-Press*'s scrutiny continued in October 2003, with coverage of the attendance by five Episcopal church members at an "Anti-Gay Confab" in Plano, Texas. The attending members included Yates, who was networking with the traditionalist American Anglican Council. In January 2005, Benton recapped a national magazine story with the headline, "*Newsweek* Outs Falls Church Episcopal as GOP Lair." Yates was linked to high-level members of the George W. Bush administration, including Attorney General Alberto Gonzales and CIA director Porter Goss. A week later, Yates replied that he was "glad to be 'on the map'" with a "hot church" but noted that Falls Church Episcopal has 3,600 worshipers from both parties, and "all are welcome." Benton's blasts at traditional Christian resistance to gay life prompted a 2001 letter from Anthony and Dianne Falzarno, who said that while they like the *News-Press*, they won't sit back while Benton "continues to take jabs at the conservative Catholic/ Protestant churches and their belief system."

What would become the paper's biggest story broke in 2006, when Falls Church Episcopal began a set of reactions protesting the election of New Hampshire reverend Gene Robinson, who was openly gay, as a bishop in 2003. The news divided the Falls Church parish, and when Reverend Yates condemned the action as being against biblical teachings, large numbers of gay-tolerant parishioners left for other places of worship. The diocese, under Bishop Peter Lee, voted to approve the ordination of Robinson. (Lee, a longtime friend of Yates, was quoted as saying he hoped they all could "be a united church while sharing and respecting our differences.")

Many of those who remained at Falls Church Episcopal, feeling their biblical teachings threatened, linked up with ten likeminded conservative churches, such as the historic Truro Church in Fairfax County. Yates helped align them with antigay Archbishop Peter Akinola of Nigeria. There was also resistance to elevating women as priests. This faction made a bold plan: in November 2006, the *News-Press* reported, the vestry voted 15–2 to leave the Virginia Diocese. A similar vote by the congregation then passed by a wide margin. And under the name of the Church of Nigeria North American Mission (CANA), the congregation would claim the historic Falls Church land on East Fairfax Street. "Episcopal Church Faces Fight to Keep Property after Voting to Exit Denomination," read the November 23, 2006 headline. "Storm clouds gather over what may become an historic fight."

The litigation over the land and revenues lasted for six years. The internet delivered the *News-Press*'s up-close coverage worldwide. Benton published numerous letters from church members of both camps. A December 28, 2006 message from Paul Brockman of Albemarle County, Virginia, argued that Falls Church Episcopal, for most of its history, was a "separate parish without the Diocese" and that prior to 1830, it was in the Fairfax Parish. Stephen Hill, in the same issue, blasted the *News-Press*'s coverage, saying it "demands an impossibly high level of civic-mindedness."

The paper did use blunt language about "homophobes" with "suspect motives" and "a simple case of trespassing." In an editorial titled "A Descent into the Abyss," in the December 14, 2006 issue, Benton wrote, "The action of the Falls Church Episcopal leadership, and that of Truro Church of Fairfax and some others across the United States, is a mild replay of the same sad history of centuries of division, slaughter, discord and tyranny within Christendom."

In a February 1, 2007 editorial titled "The Real Falls Church," Benton wrote of "many reasons to applaud" the tough stand by the Virginia bishop, which included the defrocking of Yates and twenty other traditionalist clergy, who represented about eight thousand of the roughly ninety thousand Episcopalians in the state.

Benton praised the hospitality extended to the adrift Episcopalians (those turned off by Yates's traditionalism) by nearby Falls Church Presbyterian. (Led by Chief Warden Bill Fetsch, that church's congregation included Falls Church mayor Robin Gardner and former school superintendent Warren Pace.) "Without access to our church building, we met in the living room of our home on a frigid Sunday in January 2007," recalled Robin Fetch. "An Episcopal navy chaplain came and oversaw our first service."

The *News-Press* thundered, "The tiny city of Falls Church has been assailed for years by the arrogance of those in the leadership of the Falls Church Episcopal, now rightfully called 'The Nigerians.'" Benton counseled the community to "affirm religious freedom" and "let the world know who we are through economic development."

But the editor was accused of "journalistic bullying" in a February 8, 2007 letter from Peter Davis, a reader of the paper since the age of eight. He was "excited to see a fresh stack of *Falls Church News-Press*'s bringing me and my fellow classmates the news of our fair city. However, several other residents and I have been disappointed by a disturbing trend in recent editions" on both the topic of development and the conflict over Falls Church Episcopal. "The editorial pages have spilled into the reporting."

Yates challenged Benton in a May 10, 2007 letter. "I am sorry to say you have seriously misrepresented me and the Falls Church [in a news brief].… You accuse me of labeling as non-believers those from our congregation who have chosen not to disassociate from the Episcopal Church and instead to still continue to worship as Episcopalians. They are not non-believers but our friends and fellow believers. We have simply reached different conclusions about the Episcopal Church." Benton, who occasionally mentioned his own master's degree in divinity and his attendance at the First Congregational United Church of Christ in Washington, D.C., said he apologized if some comments taken from a transcript were misunderstood.

Carol Jackson, the housing and preservation activist who stayed with Falls Church Episcopal's traditionalist faction, recalled in 2022 that the fight over the gay bishop and the church land ownership was "the only thing" she and Benton were "never compatible on. He has a style of editorializing that likes to stir up controversies," she said. She could "never get him to see more gray than black and white," though over the years, they talked things out, and she admired him.

The legal fight between the diocese and the Nigerian faction CANA, beginning in the summer of 2007 in Fairfax Circuit Court, bounced between venues. "If the court eventually rules in favor of the Diocese and the national Episcopal Church, an orderly transition with respect to all property would ensue," read the news story in August 2007. "The Church and the Diocese would retain the right, under those circumstances, to seek an accounting of all monies spent by the departed congregations and bring the individual vestry members and clergy back into litigation for that purpose."

The Fairfax Circuit Court granted the traditionalist "defectors" the right to occupy the Falls Church and other churches in the Episcopal Diocese of Virginia where similar events had occurred, based on an interpretation of a Civil War–era so-called 57–9 statute. But the Virginia Supreme Court, in June 2010, overturned that lower court ruling and remanded the matter for further consideration. The traditionalists, knowing their cause would take years to achieve, appealed to the U.S. Supreme Court. Yates said that, despite the disagreements between his breakaway CANA group and the Episcopalians still in the diocese, "this does not mean that we cannot respect each other's various viewpoints or be friends. But neither can we gloss over our…major doctrinal differences."

In March 2014, the high court declined to hear the appeal, thus finalizing the case: the traditionalists would now abandon their claim to the historic Falls Church land. After holding a final service in May 2012, those defectors reflected on having spent $2 million in a losing battle. Yates's onetime assistant Judy Thomsen said, "We were doing this for the sake of the Bible.…Maybe that's why the sermons got even better after we lost the property." The traditionalists formed their own church, Falls Church Anglican, in a large new building on Arlington Boulevard in Fairfax. Their website borrows the history of George Washington's former church. The restored congregation on the historic downtown site went on to welcome gay parishioners. In October 2022, retired bishop Gene Robinson himself made a triumphant visit for a Saturday service.

Falls Church's namesake church was far from the city's only historic place of worship, and the *News-Press* regularly reported on clergies' comings and goings and building expansions. Columbia Baptist on North Washington Street traces its founding to 1856 by seven abolitionists, as the *News-Press* noted in a January 2021 story on the church's expansion of its sanctuary. "The first building was built in 1857, right next to the original chapel of Falls Church Episcopal," the church recounted, citing a photograph by famed photographer Mathew Brady. Parishioner John Read made history in 1864, during the Civil War, when, as a Union sympathizer, he was killed by Mosby's Rangers. (Today, a downtown apartment complex bears his name.) In October 1999, the *News-Press* published a photograph of fourteen Columbia Baptist Church parishioners who went on a mission to Russia for seventeen days. The current suburban-style Columbia Baptist building, constructed in the 1950s, was outfitted in 2022–23 with a relocated skyline spire and a large new sanctuary to accommodate crowds.

Across North Washington Street lies the similarly venerable Crossman Church. These Methodists, originally meeting in the eighteenth century in a private home near today's Seven Corners, were divided during the Civil War. Seventeen members who opposed slavery split and formed Crossman Methodist Episcopal Church. It was named for Isaac Crossman (1824–1900), a civic and farming leader who donated the land for the church (his name

Columbia Baptist, now on North Washington Street, dates to 1856 and the abolitionist movement. In 2023, it was expanding with a new sanctuary. *Mary Riley Styles Library.*

is also on a Falls Church park). The first building was consecrated in 1876. In 1951, the church, having just merged with Arlington-based Christ United Methodist Church, purchased land on East Columbia Street to build a new sanctuary. Isaac Crossman's daughter Susie donated adjoining land, and construction of the modern building was completed in 1965. The *News-Press*, in December 2017, showcased Crossman's live Nativity scene and petting zoo, set to carols performed by the George Mason High School band.

The Dulin Methodist Church on East Broad Street dates to 1869, its stained-glass window sponsored by prominent Arlington military officer Henry Febrey (1828–1881). The *News-Press*'s coverage in 1995–96 dramatized the church's efforts to aid the homeless. The plan to set up a shelter on church property drew complaints from neighbors. The project required an ordinance from the city council, which was denied in December 1995. "What Child Is This?" asked Benton's editorial. "The minute political expediency, or 'cost benefit' factors, begin to enter in to determining how much attention and care we offer human beings, then we can never know how much and care we offer human beings, then we can never know how many of the world's most important people we're surely denying."

The issue festered through another winter. In an October 3, 1996 editorial, Benton wrote, "Dulin deserves a chance to perform its ministry." This drew praise in a letter from Phil Hannum, which said, "It is refreshing to read such opinions in a format which many would like to keep sterile and secular." There was talk of litigation. But the council voted 4–3, the paper reported on October 17, to side with the neighbors and block the shelter from opening. St. James Catholic Church, its attached K–8 school on West Broad Street regularly covered in the weekly paper, traces its roots to 1873. Bishop James Gibbons, the ordinary of Richmond, responding to a Northern Virginia Catholics' petition, established a mission in Falls Church to serve as an outpost of Alexandria's St. Mary's Parish. "For the next 18 years," a church history notes, "Jesuit priests traveled from St. Mary's by horse or train every three weeks to celebrate Mass in a white clapboard mission church built by parishioners in 1874—complete with a 66-ft. steeple." St. James was recognized in 1892—the only Catholic church between St. Mary's and West Virginia's St. Peters—the modern Falls Church building dating to the late 1940s.

Falls Church Presbyterian, home to the frequently photographed Scout Troop 895, was featured during Christmas 1999 for its visits from live llamas that were part of the worldwide Heifer Project, which bestows the gift of animals on the poor. In 2001, the paper reported on the church's approval of same-sex unions. First Christian Church, founded in 1952 in Arlington before moving to Leesburg Pike, drew coverage in May 1999 with its appointment of a new pastor, Jeff Timm. It is now active in aiding the homeless and providing child care.

The greater area's Jewish community inspired a June 11, 1998 headline: "Joyous Groundbreaking Fête at the Temple Rodef Shalom." Benton covered the synagogue on Westmoreland Street when Rabbi Laszlo Berkowits retired after thirty-five years and was replaced by Rabbi Amy Schwartzman. The nationally known King David Memorial Gardens, a Jewish cemetery alongside the larger grounds of National Memorial Park, located south of the city on Lee Highway, was cited when famed National Basketball Association coach Red Auerbach, who was Jewish, was buried there in November 2006.

Pioneer churches in the historically Black neighborhood off Annandale Road include Galloway United Methodist Church and Second Baptist, profiled in 2023 by the newspaper. A smaller church of some 150 largely Black congregants called Christian Way Baptist, which resided down the hall from one incarnation of *News-Press* offices, was written up in July 2003 under the headline "Worshipping in a Small Place Is Still Worship." The Christian Science faith retains a reading room centrally located at 123 Little Falls Street.

Latinos in Falls Church congregate at both the Iglesia Adventista de Falls Church on East Broad Street and La Iglesia Episcopal De Santa Maria in Fairfax on Arlington Boulevard.

The Islamic presence in the Little City was brought home after the September 11, 2001 terrorist attacks. The *News-Press*'s March 21, 2002 headline, "Feds Raid Here," covered the U.S. Customs Service, with 150 agents in Northern Virginia, entering the Council for Islamic Organizations. The Islamic group's spokesman warned of a "hostile and chilling impact," while Representative Jim Moran decried "Cowboy-Like U.S. Customs Raids on Islamic Sites." The paper's coverage of more tranquil activity included the January 2004 move of the Muslim Halalco Supermarket from the Southgate Shopping Center to Hillwood Avenue.

A December 28, 2018 photograph feature on the Dar Al-Hijrah Islamic Center at Seven Corners congratulated the women who'd graduated from a sewing academy that outfits them with a marketable skill and a machine. And on August 18, 2021, that mosque was credited in the headline "Islamic Relief USA Provided Halal Meat at Dar-Al-Hijrah Islamic Center," just outside a community known for three hundred years as Falls Church.

9

Getting Around the Little City

With walkability between home and commerce, two Metro stations, regional bus services, three major auto dealers, fifteen service stations and five body shops, Falls Church offers an array of transport options.

Its historic main intersection, however, at Broad and Washington Streets, has long been feared for its heavy pass-through traffic and history of collisions. "Condemned to Repeat," scolded the *News-Press* editorial from July 11, 1996, responding to two crashes on a Sunday involving police chases and outsiders.

The city averages ten automotive collisions with pedestrians or cyclists per year, according to a planning office report released in November 2022. As the city council considered whether to take advantage of a new state law and lower speed limits, the report estimated that of "citizens hit by a moving vehicle, if that vehicle is traveling at 23 miles per hour, 10 percent will be killed. If the speed is 32 miles per hour, then 25 percent of those hit will die. And, if the vehicle is moving at 50 miles per hour, not that uncommon even on residential streets in Falls Church, a stunning 75 percent of those hit will die."

And like car-clogged urban and suburban communities nationwide, the Little City, in the past three decades, has experimented with efforts to encourage use of public transportation.

News stories in the late 1990s focused on various experiments. In November 1996, the city council voted to close one lane at the intersection of Broad and Washington Streets during rush hour, a one-week test of an

The W&OD Bridge, dedicated by the Virginia Transportation Department and NOVA Parks in March 2021, provided safety at the Arlington border for walkers and cyclists. *Author's collection.*

effort to improve safety and boost nearby businesses, which included Brown's Hardware, Ireland's Four Provinces, Dominion Camera and Direct Jewelry Outlet. A week later, the plan was dropped.

In November 1999, the council embarked on a plan to spend $900,000 on a photographic detection system to catch red light violators; in December, it inked a three-year deal with the Nestor Firm. The system would go into effect in June 2001, using video enforcement to impose $50 fines for speeders. The installation didn't go well. "Chaos on Broad Street," stated the February 22, 2001 story, which reported a power outage for nine blocks affecting five thousand customers. A water main/pothole contractor, it was learned, had severed telephone lines, just as Nestor was installing the system. In 2010, the cameras were added at the intersections at East Broad and Cherry Streets and West Broad Street and Annandale Road. By the end of the decade, the system was helping police issue three to five hundred citations for speeding monthly.

Encouraged by dangled federal funds, several influencers in Falls Church, including the *News-Press*, in 1999, began pushing for the construction of a light rail system to reduce the number of automobiles going up and down on Broad Street. Mayor Dan Gardner was in favor, and Benton's October 7 editorial touted the $26.7 billion twenty-year plan, saying it "would certainly stimulate new economic vitality in the city's downtown." But a preliminary Virginia Transportation Department hearing that September drew only a couple of Falls Churchians. Anne Thornton, in a letter to the *News-Press*, said a brochure on light rail made her think of it as a "time bomb" and a "death knell for Falls Church as we know it."

Another experiment in the streets was the introduction of four "clean power" electric buses in July 1999, using federal funds of $2.6 million. But by November, the routes had been selected by the city planning department, and a skeptical *News-Press* commented that it "seems devoid of any clear objective." After delays, planners in May 2001 implemented a forty-five-day "do or die" test run. The July 12 issue reported, "Electric Buses Flunk Test," and the Falls Church futuristic bus became history.

But the next year, the planners made good on a new, old-fashioned, diesel-powered city bus service called George, yet another nod to George Washington. The intracity routes were rolled out in December 2002, and ridership was monitored by a nervous council, which was subsidizing the effort at eight dollars per ride. After iffy participation and opposition from City Manager Wyatt Shields, the council, in August 2010, voted 6–1 to terminate the bus system. In the paper's February 5, 1998 issue, the shuttle bus from the West Falls Church Metro to Dulles Airport was highlighted when Washington Flyer operator Farouq Massoud was named "Business Person of the Year."

If the automobile must continue to win the transportation option sweepstakes, any self-respecting community must supply available parking. Benton's long crusade for a downtown "structured parking facility," like those in Santa Barbara and Chattanooga—and a short-lived offer of federal money—dissipated due to the scarcity of land. Plus, efforts to provide on-street parking to aid merchants and customers often clash with the desire of commuters to have free lanes on which to continue moving.

But the most dramatic parking wars in the Little City have erupted over towing. Since complaints surfaced in the mid-1990s, Falls Church Police have probed to discover whether certain towing companies contracted trucks to lie in wait to swoop in within seconds to tow an errant parker, even before he's left the scene. When attendees at the annual Memorial Day parade were towed for parking in shopping strips as if they were customers, chamber of commerce executive director Stacy Hennessey, in May 2003, leveled criticism. City Attorney Ray Thorpe said predatory towers will be taken to court. A year later, Representative Jim Moran helped secure federal

Left: The localized Falls Church bus service named for George Washington ran from 2002 to 2010 before the city council grew weary of subsidizing it. *City of Falls Church.*

Below: Tow trucks infuriate Falls Churchians and untutored outsiders who get trapped after parking for holiday events. *Author's collection.*

legislation cracking down on the practice, and the city council, in September 2004, stiffened the fines, setting a thirty-minute "grace period" for risk-taking parkers. Elliott Rickenbaker complained in a January 2005 letter that he had parked in front of Dominion Camera for only fifteen minutes before the tow truck pounced. Moran's federal bill was enacted that August, authorizing a $1.72 million transportation center near the West Falls Church Metro with four hundred parking spaces, bike lockers, restrooms and water fountains at the kiss and ride. Its language against aggressive tow trucks (updated in 2016 with input from Representative Don Beyer) was paired with state laws that require a car's owner to be present during towing.

A mini drama was reported in the *News-Press* on December 8, 2005: "Eyewitness to Predatory Towing." City council members Lindy Hockenberry and Marty Meserve had ambushed a tow truck in mid-confiscation and talked the driver out of it. Meanwhile, George King, the owner of Frank's Towing Service, was arrested for tax fraud.

The *News-Press* editorialized in favor of exploring an alliance against the practice, along with experiments in "shared parking" during special events. In 2015, the city considered building a $3.4 million 109-space public parking deck near the library. But its analysis instead recommended shared parking agreements with surrounding businesses as a cheaper alternative.

Another of the parking wars broke out in 2018, after the opening of the Northside Social Restaurant at Park Avenue and North Maple Street. The coffee bar and sandwich emporium started with just a lone parking space (those nearby were used by tenants next door), which led, predictably, to a slew of unhappy parked drivers whose vehicles were towed. A broader debate unfolded in letters to the editor that September. "The people within a half-mile of the new projects at West Broad and Park Ave. and East Broad and Route 29 are probably not going to be happy with all the parking in their neighborhoods," noted Barb Molino. The issue reached school parents. "There is a lot of discussion about ours being an urban school and an urban walkable community, so we can get by with less parking," wrote Steve and Laurie Clark. "But if we can't get adults to walk a few blocks from their home to Northside Social, then why would we expect a family of five to walk a mile to go to the 1st grade concert or a rec basketball game at the high school?" "How much more traffic can North/South Washington Street take before it and Broad Street become like midtown Manhattan?" protested S.H. King. "We are no longer the 'Little City.'"

Early in the debate, Northside co-owner Brian Normile was quoted in the *News-Press* as saying it was the responsibility of guests to find their own parking places. Some patrons decided they would now avoid the restaurant. But Sally Cole, the executive director of the chamber of commerce, said the city should have taken more steps to address the issue prior to Northside opening. "It's the City's responsibility. The City did that. You can't blame Northside," Cole told the *News-Press* in August 2018.

By the end of the year, Northside management had announced the restaurant had acquired ten parking spots from nearby Park Towers Condominiums. On Facebook and Instagram, Northside management said, "We have temporary signage up at the moment and will have permanent signage up in the coming weeks. It's a holiday season miracle!"

10
CRIME AND THE LAW ENFORCERS

The Little City is the scene of crimes small and large. Fluctuating crime rates, along with the heroics and tragedies confronted by the city's thirty-two police officers, are sketched in the *News-Press*'s weekly blotter—while more noteworthy dramas make the front page.

Current police chief Mary Gavin (who, in 2012, became the city's first woman in the job) worked alongside the legendary Stephen Bittle, who spent twenty-seven years in the sheriff's job (fifty-four total in service of the city, making him the longest-serving Falls Church employee, as the *News-Press* reported after his death in December 2020). Gavin made her bones as an officer in nearby Arlington, which comes in handy, because the two jurisdictions, since 1988, have shared a hybrid roster of judges for the district court and the juvenile and domestic relations court. (On certain days, the Falls Church City Council chamber becomes a courtroom. Arlington also supplies a larger jail when needed, and jury trials for Falls Church felony cases are held in Arlington.) Sheriff candidates usually run unopposed, an exception being the 1993 election, in which a still-young *News-Press* covered the three-way race between Bittle, his former deputy Howard Miller (whom he'd fired) and U.S. Capitol Police veteran Michael Morrison. Bittle survived the election, though he continued to draw occasional electoral opposition from Miller and former police officer Phil Hannum.

On Bittle's retirement, he named as his interim successor former police officer Matt Cay, who was elected on his own with 97.7 percent of the vote in November 2021. Cay had published an essay in the *News-Press* the previous May, clarifying the interlocking but distinct functions of the two departments. "The sheriff, as an elected and sworn state law enforcement official, derives the authority of the office from the Constitution of Virginia," Cay wrote. "In contrast, the director of a police department is appointed by the locality and is commonly designated as the 'chief of police' whose authority is conferred by the local government."

A minor scandal tested the sheriff's office in the late 1990s and prompted regionwide notice. Doug Tracht, a Washington-area shock jock–style deejay, famously known as "the Greaseman," had an urge to volunteer in law enforcement. Having met Sheriff Bittle in a music store in 1988, the highly paid performer—who had already been suspended once from WWDC for inappropriate on-air comments about the Martin Luther King Jr. holiday—struck a deal to take four months of training to be a part-time sheriff's deputy (a role he had played earlier in Florida). "The Greaseman Radio Personality Appointed a Sheriff's Deputy Here," read the September 11, 1997 *News-Press* headline. For two years, diverging views on the character of Doug Tracht were hashed out in the letters column. "Why did Bittle Deputize the Greaseman?" asked Kitty Butler in letter that October, recalling an earlier "sick joke" he had told on air about date rape. Sheriff candidates Miller and Hannum chided Bittle. Then in February 1999, during his show on WARW in Bethesda, Maryland, Tracht made another attempt at a racial joke, this time about the Texas lynching victim James Byrd. Bittle then had little choice but to sever ties. Though *News-Press* reader Kathryn Pleasant wrote a letter "in defense of the Greaseman" for his talent and volunteer generosity, the April 1999 letter from Miller declared with more finality that "Hiring Tracht Was Mistake in First Place."

The newspaper became the reader's eye on city crime rates, which are influenced by tough-to-control factors, such as the state of the economy and outside influences. An editorial pushing "bolder" development in November 1994 included rising crime among reasons for "economic revitalization." Crime rises at times of change and growing pains. For example, the arrival of the Vietnamese-run shopping mall called the Eden Center

Shock jock Doug Tracht, who told controversial jokes on the radio, was fired as a Falls Church sheriff's deputy in February 1999. *Joe Lange collection.*

on the Falls Church side of Seven Corners drove several early *News-Press* crime stories. "Police Chief [Robert] Murray Plans to Step Up City Patrols at Troubled Eden Center," read the September 22, 1994 banner headline. The following February 2 issue reported that Falls Church Police, with help from an FBI task force, arrested a man at an Asian billiards club for attempted second-degree murder with a firearm. More tensions in that community emerged in February 2006, when two men were shot outside the Bangkok Vientiane restaurant at 3:00 a.m. on a Sunday. In March 1995, the paper reported on the murder—in the treasured Cherry Hill Park—of a twenty-one-year-old woman named Michele Lynn Cosbey from upper-body trauma. In May 1994, the grim headline declared, "Two Dead in Apparent Murder-Suicide at S. Washington St. Parking Lot."

In 1999, the city saw the first police shooting of a suspect in half a century. The *News-Press* reported in January that Officer Alan Freed was in good condition—thanks to his bulletproof vest—after confronting and taking out the armed and violent suspect who was spray-painting an un-plated Ford Tempo behind Trak Auto at Falls Church Plaza. Coverage in the September 14, 2006 issue hailed Deputy Sheriff Michael Wood's heroic move in using his vehicle to halt a car-jacking suspect (alleged robber Marian McDougal, twenty-four) during a dangerous ride on West Broad Street. "Moments earlier, the suspect had assaulted two Fairfax County police officers."

But for most stories, the gist was positive. "Falls Church Touts Greatest Decrease in Serious Crime," read the headline in a June 20, 1996 story reporting on a 29 percent drop in the city's crime rate, the most among eighteen area jurisdictions. "Serious Crime down 20 percent in City," the paper reported on April 10, 1997. Two years later, the drop was 11 percent, "but juvenile misdemeanors up sharply," the paper stated, specifying that incidents of public drunkenness had risen from 119 to 159 over the previous year. "Crime Rate Down, Despite Shortage of Police Officers," stated the December 2, 1999 story, chiding Murray for having given the *News-Press* a drop of only 20 percent. Youth crime continued to be news fodder in December 2001, when three George Mason High seniors were arrested at a 7-11 store after they were caught on video posing as fake panhandlers to intimidate and rob customers. In the February 7, 2002 issue, the *News-Press* reported that the seniors—two of whom had been kicked off the basketball team—had inspired a petition, signed by 263 students, to reinstate them. The *News-Press* editorial "Crime and Punishment" urged Principal Robert Smee to do so. (He did not.) The April 11 issue reported that prosecutors had dropped the felony charge against the oldest student "panhandler,"

Falls Church police battle fluctuating rates of home-grown and regional crime, despite occasional staff shortfalls and iffy equipment. *Author's collection.*

reducing it to a misdemeanor and giving him twenty days in jail and two hundred hours of community service.

The police handling of that strange episode came just months after the 9/11 terrorist attacks on New York's World Trade Center and the Pentagon in nearby Arlington. Hurried into the September 13, 2001 *News-Press* was a photograph and headline: "Falls Church's Swift, Coordinated Response to Assist Rescue Effort," which reported that the police chief, squad cars, mayor, vice-mayor and Falls Church rescue units were among first to arrive at the flaming Pentagon. When an array of responders handled a major storm in August 2003, Benton had to publish an editorial apologizing for not sufficiently crediting the sheriff's department and other auxiliary police for their role.

Another federal intervention occurred in August 1994, when one of Falls Church's abortion providers, at 101 West Broad Street, was victimized by arsonists using a dry chemical. U.S. attorney general Janet Reno put that women's health clinic and eleven others under armed guard by U.S. marshals. Falls Church police chief Murray wrote a letter saying the fire had been "observed by a citizen who flagged Sgt. Kevin McCormick, then the Arlington firefighters and the Bureau of Alcohol, Tobacco, Firearms and Explosives." In February 1998, a fire was set at the Women's Commonwealth Clinic, at 900 West Broad Street, a frequent site of antiabortion picketing. Police found burglary tools and, with the FBI, arrested thirty-eight-year-old James Anthony Mitchell of Nokesville, Virginia. An arson attack on the precious Mary Riley Styles Library was reported in January 2002. It was thought the damage to the building was limited to $40,000, and damage to the holdings cost $10,000. The drama for the *News-Press* came when ten-year-old Safe Dever was credited for reporting the blaze to his mother, who alerted librarians.

A youth tragedy covered in detail by the *News-Press* was the shooting in June 2005 of Jack "Steve" Cornejo, who had been the captain of George Mason High's 2000 state champion soccer team. The mysterious gunfire from behind the Fair Oaks Apartment complex in the county was left frustratingly unexplained by police for months. The killer, said to be Brandon Paul Gotwalt, wasn't identified until March 2007. At a trial in which Gotwalt was sued for wrongful death, a jury awarded $2 million to the Cornejo family based on an eyewitness account. But the Fairfax prosecutors pursued no criminal charges, prompting letters to the editor in protest and Mayor Robin Gardner urging Fairfax to probe further.

News-Press coverage often expanded outside the city limits, as it did in December 2005, when Fairfax police drew criticism for an allegedly slow response to a fatal car crash on Haycock Road that killed twenty-eight-year-old John Serumgard. In August 2006, the paper reported on Falls Church native (and Mason class of '92 member) Lance Guckenberger's heroics as a Fairfax police officer when he confronted gunfire at a robbery at Bailey's Crossroads. Citing regional threats of criminal youth gangs, *News-Press* reporter Darien Bates, in 2004, wrote a feature asking, "Is FC Doing Enough to Prevent Gangs?"

And the paper covered administrative issues and published photographs of performance awards. But it reported less positively on morale issues, as evidenced in the April 16, 1998 letter to the city council from Policeman Fernando Navarette asking for a pay hike. He noted a survey that citizens gave the police high marks, yet Falls Church pay is "among the very lowest in the metro area." The police union, in September 2005, complained about the "poor performance" of its pistol, the Sig Sauer P220, prompting a complaint from City Manager Daniel McKeever that he had not been alerted. In January 2007, a $10 million lawsuit by four city employees charging racial discrimination raised concerns about pay inequities and a hostile office environment. Edwin Henderson II, the president of Falls Church's Tinner Hill Foundation, wrote to the *News-Press*, "The City again faces a racial divide.…I am convinced there are enough good men and women in Falls Church to see that our community rises above the narrow boundaries of racial discrimination." One of the plaintiffs, Policewoman Derrica Wilson (the city force's first Black woman officer), stayed on the job and spoke on behalf of the department's business safety practices to the chamber of commerce. Just before the case went to trial in federal court in Alexandria, the plaintiffs, in May 2008, settled with the city for $5,000 each. And in October 2007, officer morale was reported as being "up," thanks to eleven new vehicles, including nine fully outfitted Crown Victoria cruisers.

Falls Church's white-collar crime has been more likely to bring in federal law enforcement. Todd Hitt was a superstar property developer and philanthropist who had been profiled in the *News-Press*. "Developer Todd Hitt's Commitment to Falls Church Knows No Limits," gushed the August 19, 2015 headline. The "visionary" chief of locally based Kiddar Capital was an instrumental partner in key mixed-use projects, including the refurbishment of city hall, the renovations of the high school and the Harris Teeter complex on West Broad and the coming mixed-use Whole Foods project at Washington and East Broad Streets. He was a luncheon speaker at the chamber of commerce. Hitt praised Falls Church for "good management, a city manager [Wyatt Shields] with strong business skills, a director of planning [Jim Snyder] with a very good reputation, who is very straight-forward, is creative and who really cares," he said. "Also, the city council members are smart, fair-minded and really care about Falls Church." In October 2017, the paper interviewed him in depth on his travels in a private jet to Puerto Rico to aid with flood relief. That same month, the Fairfax Arts Council named Hitt "Philanthropist of the Year."

Developer-entrepreneur Todd Hitt was riding high as a philanthropist before his 2019 guilty plea for securities fraud, resulting in him receiving six and a half years in prison. *Joanne S. Lawton* / Washington Business Journal, *copyright.*

But within a year, the law's long arm caught up with him. "F.C. Developer Todd Hitt Surrenders to FBI on Securities Fraud Charges," said the *News-Press* headline on October 5, 2018. The Justice Department put out the stunning details. The fifty-three-year-old Hitt, as reported first by *Washington Business Journal*, and his company had "falsely claimed Kiddar Capital managed $1.4 billion in assets and had offices in Houston, Palm Springs and London and failed to disclose extravagant spending, such as the leasing of private jets and the purchase of sports tickets and jewelry." The federal complaint charging eight counts of fraud alleged that Hitt had raised more than $16 million from investors by misrepresenting that he would invest $6 million in a planned $33 million purchase of a five-story building near a future Metro stop. Rather than investing the money, an affidavit alleged, Hitt, over four years, diverted funds to other projects and expenses without notifying investors. The Securities and Exchange Commission and the FBI reportedly got wind of the deeds through whistleblowers on Hitt's staff.

A week later, *News-Press* coverage stressed that Hitt's majority partner in the mixed-use project, Insight Property Group, had assured City Manager Shields that the project's construction would continue without him. Hitt was free pending trial, but his office at Broad and Washington Streets was shut down. After reaching a settlement with the SEC, Hitt appeared in Eastern Federal District Court in Alexandria in February 2019 and pleaded guilty on eight counts of securities fraud schemes that cost other companies $20 million, the *News-Press* reported. The June 21, 2019 issue reported his sentence: six and a half years in prison, plus supervised release for three years. The judge took note that Hitt's parents—owners of a prosperous construction contracting business—paid $20 million in restitution.

The crime category that attracts plenty of readers—but also poses ethical dilemmas for news editors—involves sex.

The *News-Press*'s jarring front page on February 9, 2006, announced the "Panty Raider Bust." Falls Church resident Charles Dalmas III, a CIA employee who was married with two children in the public schools, was charged with seventeen counts of robbery. He had broken into homes in nearby Fairfax and stolen cash, jewelry, antiques and some one thousand pieces of women's undergarments, which police found. His neighbors could hardly believe it, the paper reported. Dalmas would later be sentenced to twenty-four years in prison, all but three suspended, and he had to pay restitution.

Closer to home was the arrest in February 2004 of Frank Marino, a popular drama and visual arts teacher at George Mason High School. The charges said the fifty-year-old had had sexual relations with a student, aged sixteen to seventeen, over the course of a year in hotel rooms. Prince William County prosecutors filed three charges against him for committing "crimes against nature," along with three charges of taking indecent liberties with a child. The shocking news hit the high school students in the middle of their sold-out production of *Bye Bye Birdie*. Emotional student actors published statements of support for the now-suspended Marino, among them Councilman David Snyder's daughter Sarah, the *News-Press* reported. "Despite Teacher's Arrest, the Show Will Go On," read the February 19 headline. In its sympathetic editorial "Unconstitutional Charges," the paper stressed that the beloved Marino, an Agnes Meyer Outstanding Teacher Award winner, was innocent until proven guilty, and the paper was "heartened his attorney will fight."

That position was backed in only some letters to the editor. Others cited the "pain of a minor" and the need to send a message that such relations "won't be tolerated." A November 4 letter from Louise Hilsen and Donald Foley said the abuse story "lacked concern for the victim." Laura Stricker added, "Regardless of how popular the teacher was, he committed a crime against a child."

In April, prosecutors dropped the old-fashioned "crimes against nature" charge, and Marino pleaded guilty. He was sentenced to eight years in prison. In October 2015, the paper reported that Marino, having left prison in 2011, died of cancer in his home in Richmond.

An even messier case was to come. Michael Gardner was a blogger and Falls Church Democratic Party leader who was married to Mayor Robin Gardner. In November 2010, the *News-Press* took him on as a columnist, using the title "The Little City Weed." The column's style was to comment on politics irreverently. "'The Weed' is not interested in being your public servant," he wrote in his opener. "In my dotage I find myself being the rare liberal despot who eschews dog parks and finds actual conversation with voters akin to the annoyances associated with recycling."

But the unamusing headline that ran on June 24, 2011, hit a wide audience: "Michael Gardner Arrest Stuns Entire D.C. Region." The news story by Benton credited the *News-Press* for the scoop. "The arrest on Wednesday of well-known Falls Church citizen-activist Michael A. Gardner on charges of sexually abusing three young girls has shocked not only Falls Church, but the entire Washington, D.C. region, as major coverage by the area's premiere daily, *The Washington Post*, the Associated Press and at least two major television news organizations, WJLA and WUSA, has demonstrated," Benton wrote. "Unfolding, updated coverage continues to appear on the websites of these organizations in the two days since the City of Falls Church announced the arrest Wednesday afternoon, and it was first reported by the *Falls Church News-Press*."

Gardner was charged with sexually abusing three girls, two of whom, ages nine and ten, attended a birthday slumber party for his ten-year-old daughter one Saturday night. A third child, also under the age of thirteen, was allegedly abused in a separate incident. The listed charges were for aggravated sexual battery and a count of sexual penetration.

Democratic activist, columnist and parent Michael Gardner, after years of litigation, pleaded guilty to child sexual abuse in 2015. *Arlington County Sheriff's Office.*

Gardner's first attorney, former Falls Church mayor Brian O'Connor, was quoted as stating that his client denied the allegations. "I am very confident of Mr. Gardner's innocence," O'Connor said. "We think this is all a misunderstanding of some kind." He told the *News-Press* his immediate goal was to secure Gardner's release from the Arlington Detention Center. Gardner was released on a $50,000 bond.

Thus began a convoluted four-year trip through the courts, with ups and downs for Gardner, his family and some supporters who judged evidence that required interpretations of intimate DNA samples from two young girls and the accused. The *News-Press* provided steady coverage, even gaining access to sealed court papers. Gardner's defense provided character witnesses. In May 2012, after a prosecution led by Loudoun County prosecutor Alex Amato (Arlington Commonwealth's attorney Theo Stamos deferred because she knew the Gardners), an Arlington Circuit Court jury found Gardner guilty of two counts of sexual battery and one of object penetration. The jury-recommended sentence was twenty-two years in prison and a fine of $15,000.

In June 2013, Gardner's attorney appealed to a three-judge panel of the Virginia Appeals Court, which rejected the appeal. But a year later, the Virginia Supreme Court voted 6–1 to reverse the conviction, finding that Arlington Circuit Court trial judge Benjamin Kendrick was wrong to have barred two character witnesses from testifying that Gardner was a good parent. The Gardner family released a statement welcoming what they perceived as "the many errors" of the trial as they waited for a retrial. "Since the ruling fell short of finding Gardner innocent of the charges, the 'double jeopardy' rule does not apply, and the Commonwealth Attorney's Office has made it clear a new trial will ensue," the *News-Press* wrote. Gardner was released after having served two years.

Before a new trial could take place, however, the paper, on October 1, 2014, broke the astounding development that Gardner had been rearrested for felony sexual battery. The new charges, which saw him returned to the Arlington Detention Center, came from the testimony of a new alleged victim, a niece under the age of thirteen who reported a sexual assault from 2009.

With the new trial beginning in late 2015, a final dramatic event unfolded. As Benton reported in a September 24, 2015 dispatch, "Michael Gardner Pleads Guilty in 2 Child Sex Abuse Cases, Sentenced to 20 Years." The agreement, on the trial's second day, came with a sentence to serve twenty years out of a forty-year sentence, along with the requirement to register as a sex offender. Nicole Wittmann of the Commonwealth Attorney's Office said, "We are pleased that the victims have closure and finality. I'm confident that other children will be protected based on this result." Falls Church police chief Mary Gavin added, "I am very proud of all of stakeholders in the Criminal Justice System, particularly the victims in this case. The four little girls displayed tremendous courage and strength. The Falls Church Police Department is grateful to all mutual aid law enforcement partners from federal, state and local organizations."

As for the Gardner family, Michael's sister Maya Jerome gave the *News-Press* a startling statement: "It is with a heavy heart that I inform you that this afternoon Michael took a deal to protect his family. The deal ensured that Robin and the kids would remain safe and be free from prosecution. We were winning the trial....We proved that things did not happen as was being related...but when the prosecution AND the judge showed that they were willing to go after Robin with the same vitriol that they went after Michael, Michael gave them what they wanted." The Gardners' attorney Bradley Haywood added, "Based on a series of in-court rulings, Michael concluded that he could not receive a fair trial and that continued proceedings risked unfair attention and potential legal action against his family. His guilty plea therefore represented an effort to protect his wife and children, and moreover reflected a hope that finality will provide all parties involved a sense of closure and an opportunity to heal."

The *News-Press*'s coverage, while steady and detailed, cut too much slack for Gardner, according to Benton's friend and accountant Michael Diener. "Nick was very good friends with Robin and talked to her regularly," he said in a 2022 interview. "In my opinion, that blinded him to the facts, and it took him a long time to come around." But he did.

11

The Joy of Sports

Sports pages—generally the best-read (and imaginatively written) sections of a newspaper—are in the *News-Press*'s version a grab bag. Falls Church sports nuts receive a steady dose of high school coverage, combined with reporting on Little League, Babe Ruth League, college and Washington-area professional-level action—consistency depending on the enthusiasms and energies of the weekly's stretched staff.

Benton's own love for baseball—cultivated since his days playing as a scholarship-receiving college outfielder and first baseman—prompted him, during the *News-Press*'s first year, to board the unsuccessful bandwagon of locals seeking to bring a minor-league team to play on a field that was to be built near the West Falls Church Metro. In June 1991, he rented a bus and led sixty readers on a "fact-finding" trip to a Frederick, Maryland ballpark to view a model. The paper ran a "Why I Love Baseball" essay contest (the prize: tickets to Baltimore Orioles games). "Crack of the Bat" was the headline for the March 13, 2004 preview for the *News-Press*-sponsored "Day at the Ballpark" at the high school.

The mainstay, just blocks from the newspaper office, was George Mason (later Meridian) High School, which, due to its small student body, for years competed largely in Division II (the Bull Run District) sports, requiring travel for both players and reporters. Benton himself, along with Mike Hume, who was briefly the sports editor, provided much of the on-scene coverage of "Mustang Madness," traveling to Front Royal, Virginia, in February 1994 for the state basketball tournament. "Mustangs Do the

Come on Out to
News-Press Day
at the Ball Game!

Fun!
Sunshine!

Friday, May 5
5 p.m.

FREE!
Hot Dogs
Peanuts
Soda Pop
and
News-Press
Stadium Cups!

Root on the Home Team

George Mason High School
Mustangs Vs. Strasburg

GMHS Baseball Field
7124 Leesburg Pike

The entire Falls Church community is invited
& encouraged to support our school team!

Sponsored by the Falls Church News-Press with support
from the George Mason High School Boosters Club.

Early on, the *News-Press* increased its visibility by promoting a leisure event and feeding the crowd. *Author's collection.*

Bristol Stomp," read Benton's (baby boomer–centric) headline for the November 1997 girls' basketball victory in Bristol, Virginia. That same year, the boys' tennis team racked up its fourth state title. "State Soccer Title!" shouted the front page on June 4, 1998. The paper, in February 1999, profiled basketball star Jason Motlagh, who scored 613 points in three years on the varsity team (having worked at the paper, he was given a *News-Press* college scholarship). The paper also followed the professional baseball career of Eddie Jordan, class of '97, who was named All-Metropolitan. In fifteen games his senior year, he batted .590, with 4 homers and 35 stolen bases, while winning four games as a pitcher. He went on to play for George Mason University and then for the Orioles farm team in 2001 (the statistics for which the paper reported from Sarasota, Florida).

March 2001 saw the boys' hoopsters win the regionals championship and entering the state tournament. "Recalling 1966: The Last Time Mustang Team Made It to States," read Benton's three-quarter-page feature that included an interview with retired coach Ed Sommer on how his team lost by one point to Albemarle County in the University of Virginia gym. "Mustangs Pull Away in Fourth Period Again, Beat Arcadia 67–50 in State Quarter Final," read the March 15, 2001 coverage. For the finals, however, with star shooter Nate Hamme suffering a twisted ankle, the report was titled, "Mustangs Valiant in State Final Loss." The team lost to Radford High School, 83–63, despite Kenny Wilson's 31 points to end "a storybook season." Benton also played defense for student sports fans when, in October 1997, the referee at a hoops game grew annoyed with the heckling by one or two in the bleachers. He ordered the stands emptied of twenty students, including a reporter who promoted the editorial titled "Civil Liberties," warning of a danger to student rights. The *News-Press* gave generous coverage to Fairfax-based Thomas Jefferson Science and Technology High School basketball star Noah Kramer-Dover (a Falls Church resident and son of former mayor Dale Dover) in February 1998, when the Naval Academy–bound senior scored his one thousandth point.

All in all, the Mustangs, as of this writing, have won three Division II state titles in girls' basketball, eleven state championships in boys' soccer (Groups A, 2A and 3), fourteen Group A titles in boys' tennis, five Group 2A state championships in girls' soccer, four titles in girls' cross-country and one title in girls' lacrosse. The arrival of lacrosse at the high school drew front-page *News-Press* coverage in March 2004.

In November 2002, the paper covered the football team's first game after the dedication of the athletic fields following a $2.5 million renovation. And sentimentally, the *News-Press* also chronicled the high school alumni basketball games back in the old gym. The paper broadened its lens to cover nearby Falls Church High School (in Fairfax) when it lost to George Mason in football in the September 2004 Outback Bowl, 22–18. It showcased the McLean High School girls' softball team's victory in the World Series in Waco, Texas. Benton even covered the hot dog eating contest at the annual Spring Day at the Ball Park—the record as of May 2003 was fifteen.

To cover Falls Church's Kiwanis Little League baseball and soccer, plus youth recreation league hoops, the *News-Press* relied primarily on volunteer parental scribes. It reported the untimely death, in May 1996, of primo soccer coach Larry Graves, for whom an area soccer field was later named. When State Delegate Bob Hull, in January 2006, proposed legislation, his "Home Security and Tranquility Act," to reduce noise from the playing fields that bothered the neighbors, he had to withdraw after a backlash— Fairfax Superintendent Gerry Connolly said it would take 286 fields out of play.

George Mason (now Meridian) High School athletes, fans and cheerleaders drew plenty of coverage in the weekly paper. *From the* News-Press.

The paper's steady coverage of high school sports was reinforced with this scoreboard logo. *From the* News-Press.

The area's on-field dramatics included twin phenomena in the summer of 2005. "Falls Church Little Leaguer Records Rare Unassisted Triple Play," Mike Hume reported in the paper's May 26 issue. Eight-year-old Billy Smith, the third basemen for the Mudcats, caught a line drive with the bases loaded and tagged out two runners. Astonishingly, on June 9, the paper reported, nine-year-old Harry Slonin, the third baseman for the Alley Cats, caught a pop-up and also completed a triple play. When the Falls Church eleven- to twelve-year-old baseball team called the Red traveled to Newport News, Virginia, that July, parent Phil Duncan (a future councilman) reported on how his son's team beat Essex County 2–0, as pitcher Lansing Veeder threw a perfect game. To round out that hot summer, in August, when the nearby McLean Little League girls' team made the World Series in Portland, Oregon, Hume traveled there to write up and photograph their 6–2 victory over kids from Orange, Connecticut. And in July 2003, the paper covered the all-stars from the Falls Church–Annandale Babe Ruth League Virginia state baseball champions as they headed to Alabama for nationals (and lost 2–1). In a nod to small-town intimacy, the paper devoted two pages in its March 29, 2001 issue to photographs and the results of Falls Church Recreation and Parks Department basketball. In September 2004, the paper gave a special byline to ten-year-old Zachary Diener's interview with Atlanta Braves outfielder Chipper Jones during a trip to the Pittsburgh stadium.

College basketball drew *News-Press* coverage on special occasions. In March 2002, the March Madness NCAA Tournament games were staged in downtown Washington, D.C., at the MCI Center. Sitting through four games on a Saturday, Benton wrote, "is not something you get to do every day." (He would travel again, in April 2003, to the Final Four in New Orleans, where he interviewed University of Kansas All-American Nick Collison.) And in March 2006, the Falls Church paper horned in on the national coverage of the Cinderella story–like rise of George Mason University's basketball team. The Fairfax college was unfamiliar to many outside the Mid-Atlantic states. "GMU Is Us," read Benton's editorial, which observed that, "finally, people are discovering just how the extended the reach of the university has become in the region." Hume recapped the university's sports history, going back to 1966, when the fledgling team played against Lorton Prison inmates. And he journeyed to Indianapolis in April for the Final Four, in which the Mason men lost to the University of Florida.

Indiana University's famously ill-tempered coach Bobby Knight prompted a judgmental column from Mike Hoover in May 2000. And at

A boyhood connection allowed Benton to access the Baltimore Orioles ballfield to commune with pitcher Jesse Orosco in 1995. *From the* News-Press.

the professional level, Benton met Washington Bullets tallman (seven feet, eight inches) Gheorghe Muresan at the White House Correspondents' Dinner in May 1999 and invited him for an appearance at the low-ceilinged *News-Press* office.

Major-League Baseball—always a reader favorite—was the topic when Benton made a sentimental journey to Detroit in September 1999 to witness the demolition of the old Tiger Stadium, "a national treasure." Through a personal contact from his playing days, Benton hosted and interviewed Milwaukee pitcher Jesse Orosco in July 1995. The *News-Press*'s "My Sporting View" column allowed free roaming for Benton and Hume, who vented entertainingly on the perennially hapless Chicago Cubs and the rise of NBA wonder LeBron James. Hume's own "Picking Splinters" column profiled the Georgetown University Hoyas basketball team's heroics and described a March 2005 trip to spring training in Fort Lauderdale, Florida, for the brand-new Washington Nationals.

Figure skating, which draws nowhere near the audience of the big three men's sports, attracted Benton. In January 2004, he began what became a series with a "My Sporting View" on nineteen-year-old Johnny Weir, whose victory in Atlanta he called "one of the decade's great Sports

Stories." By March, the *News-Press* had published an exclusive interview with the sometimes-eccentric athlete. The three-time national figure skating champion was covered with datelines the next year in Portland, Oregon, and in Saint Louis in 2006. A photograph of him sporting a fur coat prompted Benton's description him as "a role model for 'different, stifled, squelched.'" Having come out as gay, Weir, in 2012, was given his own *News-Press* column for a year.

12

Beyond the White Males

The *News-Press* staff, over the decades, has been mostly white. Reporter Drew Costley, a Black man from a prominent Arlington family, was a news editor from 2014 to 2016 (he went on to be a climate reporter for the Associated Press), and the current circulation manager, Julio Idrobo, is Latino. Mastheads show that not quite half the paper's jobs have gone to women.

But the *News-Press*'s coverage of a Virginia community with a long and detailed history of racial tension has been steady and modernized, if not universally praised. A highlight came in the autumn of 2005 with a two-part series by Darien Bates, resurrecting forgotten details of how Falls Church schools were put on the road to integration in the 1950s. The "unsung hero" of the story was John A. Johnson, a white school board member and air force veteran who wrote a letter advocating for the inclusion of "negroes" in mainstream schools. The Falls Church board declined to forward the letter to the state board of education at a time of Virginia's "massive resistance" to U.S. Supreme Court–ordered integration. (He moved to Arlington and became general counsel of NASA.) The second part of the series profiled H.P. "Duke" Strople, the board's most active defender of segregation (he spoke so long at meetings, the other members imposed a time limit), along with Marian Costner, the first Black graduate of George Mason High School (class of '64).

The central tale of race in Falls Church—the 1915 formation of the first rural NACCP branch, accomplished at Tinner Hill on South Washington

Street to counter segregated zoning in housing—gets repeated in periodic coverage. The leaders of the group were stonemason Joseph Tinner (1875–1928) and Dr. Edwin B. Henderson (1883–1977), whose grandson Edwin Henderson II remains active in preserving Black history, education, sports and the popular annual Tinner Hill Music Festival. Homes occupied by Black families that were built in the area during the early twentieth century used historic bricks from the two-centuries-old Big Chimneys house, which was demolished in 1914.

As early as November 1993, the *News-Press* reported on the city's designation of the Henderson house at 307 South Maple Street, the first rural office of the NAACP, as historic. In April 1998, the paper also cooperated with the foundation in sponsoring a letters to the editor contest for eleven-to eighteen-year-olds, a tribute to the fact that Edwin Henderson, early in the twentieth century, published nearly three hundred such letters. Edwin Henderson II also drew mentions for the nomination of his grandfather to the National Basketball Association Hall of Fame, which covers professional Black athletes, and his work with young Black men chronicled in a 1939 book, *The Negro in Sports*.

On Tinner Hill itself, the paper covered the October 1999 dedication of the *Arch of Welcome* monument (built in part with a $4,000 donation from the Wallenberg Foundation and designed by John Ballou). The paper profiled George Tinner, who worked in Arlington and Fairfax Counties. A photograph showed stonemasons assembling the pink granite, with Tinner and Henderson descendants, along with volunteer history activist Dave Eckert, the vice-president of the Tinner Hill Heritage Foundation. Also set in motion by the city council was an initial $150,000 for the creation of a Tinner Hill Education Center near the site. (That project has not yet materialized. Henderson, in a 2022 interview, cited a downturn in the economy, parking limits and disagreements over a feasibility study for the delay. It still could happen.) What did materialize in 2016 was a sidewalk step-by-step timeline showcasing civil rights history in Falls Church, which—situated on South Washington Street outside the 455 at Tinner Hill Apartments—leads up to the Tinner Hill monument. It was the brainchild of Nikki Graves Henderson and was organized by the Tinner Hill Heritage Foundation, the Falls Church Historical Commission and the Arts and Humanities Council.

Overall, the history of the civil rights movement in Falls Church has been a "fairly omitted unknown topic that I felt needed to be brought to light," Edwin Henderson II said in a 2022 interview. "Few people knew there was a civil rights history the city could proud of. It's very important to have a local

Democratic senator Mark Warner honors Martin Luther King Jr. Day at the Tinner Hill Archway in 2022. *Gary Mester, for the* News-Press.

rag to cover the many topics Nick Benton does," he added. "Even if he doesn't get all the facts correct, it's not worth dickering about. I've had occasion to go back to add my own to stories that Nick or other reporters have done." In February 2023, the paper broke fresh news on the location of racist covenants in residential property deeds in early-twentieth-century Falls Church.

The *News-Press* also covered more traditional history, such as its May 1999 feature on Civil War Day, which included details on the role of the local Taylor's Tavern during the war. Actors dressed as Abraham Lincoln and Robert E. Lee and nineteenth-century reel dancers. That September, the paper ran photographs of first annual Colonial Church and Tavern Day, where actors dressed as Natives at Big Chimneys Park. For Black History Month that February, the *News-Press* covered Black broadcaster Tavis Smiley's appearance at the State Theatre, and under its "Models of Excellence" label, the paper profiled veteran Jewish broadcast journalist Herbert Kaplow and his reporting on civil rights struggles going back to the 1950s.

Homier coverage came in an August 1994 feature, "The Remarkable Life of Callie Mae Haskins," who was born the daughter of enslaved people in 1910 in Milton, South Carolina, and then retired at Falls Church's Winter Hill condos.

A civil rights–themed march on Martin Luther King Jr. Day passes by the Bowl America lanes. *Gary Mester.*

Falls Church is 76.4 percent white; 4.7 percent black; .02 percent American Indian; 9.2 percent Asian; and 10.7 percent Latino, according to 2020 census figures. The paper's readers would be accustomed to seeing Dale Dover, the city's first Black mayor (voted by council 1990), and architect Alan Brangman, a Black leader who won a council seat in 1994 with the Falls Church Citizens Organization and was mayor in 1996–98. By 2000, the city's communications director was Dionne Williams, who was also Black; she left in 2005. Former deputy city manager Willie Best, who left in 2003, was also Black. The current clerk of the court is Shana Lawan Gooden, who is also Black. Nader Baroukh, of Iranian descent, was elected to city council in 2008 and was mayor from 2010 to 2014.

Latino residents show up chiefly in the paper's coverage of education, immigration and, on a lighter note, restaurants. "Computer Training Program Helps 18 Hispanic Students," wrote teacher-columnist Mike Hoover in January 1998. The program was a collaboration between Falls Church City Public Schools and Virginia Tech. During the pandemic in July 2021, the *News-Press* showcased a public library program in which volunteers taught English as a second language to recent immigrants over Zoom. And Benton wrote a review of the El Zunzal Salvadorean-Mexican

restaurant at 917 West Broad Street, profiling its musical bandstand host Marino Perdome.

Members of the Jewish community occasionally write to protest the newspaper's language they consider insensitive. In May 2005, the *News-Press* wrote up a talk by World War II army ranger Roger Neighborgall, a photograph for which showed an authentic Nazi flag. A letter from Beth Helman and Dave Rifkin chided the paper for quoting phrases such as "master race" and "chosen people." Benton replied that he could have chosen better wording than "master race" but said that a publication can still discuss causes of that great war.

Asian Americans have a highly visible presence in Falls Church. A chief reason for this was the influx of refugees from war-torn Vietnam in the late 1970s, who came first to Arlington and then migrated down Wilson Boulevard toward Falls Church. In July 2005, refugee Nguyen Van Bong, formerly of Saigon, was dramatically reburied in the National Memorial Cemetery. As early as 1993, dozens of Vietnamese merchants began opening shops in the onetime site of a Zayre's variety store, prompting guest columnist Phil Hannum to write in the February 11 issue that the site called the Eden Center "continues as an eyesore (not in my opinion), a reflection of the merchants and John Nguyen." The city had rejected a proposal to make George Mason Square an Asian center. But by March 14, 1996, the *News-*

The Vietnamese shopping strip called the Eden Center on Wilson Boulevard evolved from a high-crime area to a rich array of restaurants and Asian culture. *From the* News-Press.

Press headline said that the site was being revamped as the "Largest Mall of Its Kind in the U.S." by Florida-based shopping mall owner Norman Ebenstein. There were occasional reports of violent crimes in the area, so Ebenstein, in 1997, donated money for cameras and monitors to be placed at the nearby police substation. "Nightclubs Moved Out, Eden Center Will Become 'Family Oriented,' says Landlord."

Benton's coverage expanded to the February 17, 2005 issue's photographs of Vietnamese New Year events ("Adopted Families Celebrate Culture") and the 2006 Chinese New Year celebrations (the Year of the Dog). The paper profiled Alan Thai, a Vietnamese refugee who arrived as a "boat person," and, on a lighter note, provided a December 2004 profile of the local South Korean entrepreneur Jhoon Rhee's Tae Kuan Do martial arts studio.

Possible prejudice against a man of Arab descent emerged in September 2001, when Harold Miller, a revenue commissioner since 1990, fired auditor Sam Khamas, a fourteen-year employee, for complaining about discrimination. Miller, slated for the November ballot, allegedly used an ethnic slur and faulted Khamas for taking his complaint to the city attorney and manager but not him. Miller won reelection, but after an audit, Khamas was reinstated in January 2002.

The evolving role of women in Falls Church's public life came across in three decades of *News-Press* coverage, though the women's movement

The city's second-oldest structure was, for decades, home to the Falls Church Woman's Club, now the Center for Spiritual Enlightenment. *Author's photograph.*

was already decades in the works. The arrival of modern gender roles was captured in a February 1997 photograph that shows Falls Church women at the women's club (222 North Washington Street) jokingly reenacting a tea and fashion show chorus line that had been executed a half-century earlier by the Victorian Society of Falls Church. The earlier event was meant to raise funds for the group's clubhouse (a former city hall and library, the city's second-oldest standing building, the *News-Press* reported, after Cherry Hill farmhouse). The club's first president was Carol Manly, an editor in the 1940s of the *Falls Church Echo* (her husband, Charles, was the publisher). That building, a former church, has been the Center for Spiritual Enlightenment since the club sold it in 2003.

Also active for decades (and still so) was the Falls Church chapter of the League of Women Voters. In February 1995, the *News-Press* covered its exhibit at the community center celebrating seventy-five years of the national organization (it had been active in Falls Church for forty-four years). The local league continues to produce nonpartisan voting guides and encourage recycling. It gives an award named for its longtime leader (in the 1950s, the sole woman school board member) Jane Dexter and her husband, Wayne. In 2003, with the controversial Iraq War raging, the league encouraged the city council to pass an antiwar resolution, but it declined. Separately, in April 1996, the fortieth annual banquet for the Falls Church Business and Professional Women's Association was keynoted by Representative Jim Moran.

The city became a pioneer in individual woman leadership. When Councilwoman Robin Gardner was chosen by her colleagues to be mayor in July 2006, she became the third woman in the job, following Carol DeLong (from 1980 to 1988) and Betty Blystone (1988 to 1990). The first woman elected to the city council was Edna Clark, a former president of the chamber of commerce who died in August 2000 at the age of eighty-five, the *News-Press* reported. In 1992, the paper covered six-term Democratic state delegate Leslie Byrne being sworn in as the first woman U.S. representative in Virginia history during what was called the "Year of the Woman." (She lost to Republican Tom Davis in 1994.) In 1995, Arlington County board member Mary Margaret Whipple launched her successful bid to represent both Arlington and Falls Church in the state senate with an interview with the paper.

By 2003, the longstanding Falls Church Commission on Women, which gave out an annual Gundry Award for civic activism, felt confident enough to disband.

In current-day Falls Church, women activists and their partners conduct a springtime history walk (canceled during the 2020 pandemic), a "brainchild," as the *News-Press* reported, of the Tinner Hill Heritage Foundation, the Elected Women of Falls Church and Falls Church's Women's History

Group. The two-mile stroll, organized by Sally Ekfelt, visits Big Chimneys Park, city hall and Tinner Hill Park. It honors "grand marshals," usually educators and school volunteers, and in 2021, eighteen "Young Women of Action" were noted as student organizers of a protest following the 2020 killing of George Floyd by Minneapolis police. Women in business are celebrated, like in February 1999, when Barbara Cram, the founder of the Greenscape Garden Shop, was given the chamber of commerce's Pillar of the Community Award.

Among the frequently celebrated Falls Church women is Edna Nina Frady, who died in late November 2022 at the age of ninety. The daughter of Donald Frady, the early public works director, she was nicknamed "Boss Frady" for her influence over local Democratic nominations for state and national office. She was a member of the Falls Church Women's Club, the Village Preservation and Improvement Society, Citizens for a Better City and the Falls Church Democratic Committee. Her passing was marked by Senator Mark Warner and Representative Don Beyer. "Her strongest years in Falls Church as head of the City's Democratic Committee not coincidentally coincided with the period when Virginia shifted from a Red to a predominantly Blue state, with Northern Virginia centered around Falls Church leading the charge," Nick Benton wrote. "It began with Warner's election as governor in 2000 and continued through the two elections of Barack Obama as president of the U.S." Accounting firm executive Mike Diener added, "With all the urban development that Falls Church has gone through, Edna is the reason that we haven't lost the charm and soul or our small-town roots."

13

FALLS CHURCH FUN

On New Year's Eve 1999, the Little City's tercentennial downtown gala in the freezing wind drew four thousand celebrants to the first-ever Watch Night. The alcohol-free, all-ages event at the village's main intersection was covered by Benton as a new and lasting tradition. Closing off the intersection of North Washington and Broad Streets swelled turnout, the paper observed a year later. Food, free parking, shuttle buses and music were provided; swing bands played at the State Theatre, and bluegrass bands played at Falls Church Episcopal. By New Year's 2004, the headline over the photographs read, "New Year's Eve Was a Rockin' Good Time in Downtown FC." Supervised New Year's celebrations held at the community center for high schoolers and middle schoolers also got ink.

Through the seasons, a Valentine's Day charity dance was written up in the paper's February 4, 1993 edition, featuring Bruce Hornsby and the Range, along with Danny and the Del Notes at the community center. The 2002 "Eggscellent" Easter egg hunt became a regular *News-Press* springtime photographic feature. The Memorial Day parade became a favorite showcase for all the Little City's cast, with the *News-Press* publishing the handout program. (Benton wrote an editorial about the thrill of being a grand marshal, and since 1992, he has ridden by the hundreds of onlookers on Park Avenue in a *News-Press*-bannered convertible.) In the 2021 parade, which was altered by the pandemic, Grand Marshal Lindy Hockenberry, a retired teacher and city council member, led a phalanx of city employees in vehicles on a four-mile route that almost matched the

The New Year's Eve Watch Night gathering started during the Falls Church tercentennial year, 1999, and became wildly popular. *From the* News-Press.

The annual Memorial Day parade presents a fine chance for the newspaper staff to fly their banner. *From the* News-Press.

city's circumference. They wore cicada T-shirts featuring a big bug, which the Falls Church Education Foundation sold as part of a fundraiser for the Family Assistance Fund.

The July 4 fireworks at George Mason High School in the millennial year, 2000, covered two pages of the paper with photographs and drew a record crowd of five thousand. For the French Bastille Day on July 14, the paper photographed the traditional race between Cote d'Or restaurant waiters carrying champagne glasses on their trays. More customized to Falls Church is the annual Fall Festival at Cherry Hill Park. For the October 2003 Farm Day, the photographic essay proclaimed it was "a great day to play in the hay." And kid-friendly photographic essays appeared every Halloween under headlines such as "Hobnobbin' with Hobgoblins." At Christmastime, Santa arrives on the turret of a fire engine from the East Falls Church station.

"What a Turnout for the Thomas Jefferson Fun Fair," ran the March 1996 account of elementary school togetherness, along with write-ups of the George Mason Middle School talent show and the Saint James School bazaar. The *News-Press* even wrote up the "Home for the Holidays" gatherings of George Mason/Meridian alumni. For the business crowd, Benton gave

Above: Falls Church is home to patriotic veterans of World War II, the Korean and Vietnam Wars, as well as the actions in Afghanistan and Iraq. *From the* News-Press.

Right: Early in the paper's tenure, skilled French waiters from the Code d'Or restaurant on North Washington Street staged a Bastille Day race. *From the* News-Press.

Every Christmas brings an evening road trip by Santa, staffed by the East Falls Church Volunteer Fire Department, to every Falls Church street. *Gary Mester.*

regular coverage to allies in the chamber of commerce, whose 2001 annual fête drew a record 171 guests. And the paper ventured into nearby Bailey's Crossroads for its Community Day Fair.

Famous regionwide is the Falls Church Saturday morning farmers' market. Started in 1984 by Recreation and Parks Department director Howard Herman (a Mason High alum), its overhead street banners attracted produce, victual, craft and beverage merchants from across rural America. In May 2020, a letter to the *News-Press* from Emily Zaas read, "My husband and I own Black Rock Orchard in Lineboro, Maryland. We have been coming to the Falls Church Farmers Market to sell our fruit for more than 25 years. The market has a loyal following. Falls Church customers have shown up in the past to see us through trials of bad weather, poor crops or worker shortages." She called the institution a "jewel," and Rodale.com, in 2012, named it "one of the top Farmer's Markets in America." When Herman retired in 2011, the city proclaimed April 10 Howard E. Herman Day and named a park at the Rees-Hamlet Tract on West Broad Street Howard Herman Steam Valley Park.

The Little City is a mini music city. It boasts three major instrument stores that offer lessons—Foxes (whose owner, Jim Edmonds, was profiled in the *News-Press* when he sold the store in 2006), Action Music and, right by Seven Corners, the chain outlet Guitar Center. Not one but two recording studios serve aspiring performers—Cue Recording Studios and 38 North Studio—located a block apart. In the 1960s, the Falls Church Community Center was famous around the region for the concerts it held by national acts. Local music historian John Maier documented these performances.

But the area's two truly unique music institutions are the Tinner Hill Music Festival and the regionally popular State Theatre. What in the early years was called the Tinner Hill Blues Festival got its start as a "one-off" street concert during the 1999 tercentennial celebration, suggested by Jim Edmonds, working with principal organizers Edwin Henderson II and his wife, Nikki. The idea was to bring blues performers to the town to draw public attention to Falls Church's civil rights history centered at Tinner Hill. The group teamed with history buff Dave Eckert, who recalled, "I went to Nick Benton and said, 'Something happened here.' And we wanted to do a celebration," Eckert recalled in 2022. "He was very supportive from the get-go, and during that first year, he provided coverage. I was almost jumping for joy, it meant so much to me." To accommodate crowds, it was

The regionally influential Saturday morning Falls Church Farmers' Market was long managed by Howard Herman, the director of city recreation and parks. *Author's photograph.*

Left: Walking distance from the State Theatre are two recording studios, a musical instrument store, a ballet school and a compact-disc vendor. *Author's photograph.*

Below: Nationally known finger-picking blues guitarist John Jackson, born locally, performed at Falls Church Watch Night a year before his death in 2002. *Tinner Hill Heritage Foundation.*

Opposite: Rock bands pack them in at the renovated State Theatre, which arranged parking lot performances during the 2020–22 COVID lockdown. *Josh Brick.*

moved to Cherry Hill. It is held on the second Saturday in June, combining with history discussions and civil rights recollections to raise money for year-round research and commemorations done by the Tinner Hill Heritage Foundation. The event's performers have included Daryl Davis, Chuck Brown and Bobby Parker, with tastes of gospel and rhythm and blues.

"The music is a hook; it's a universal language," said Nikki Graves Henderson, the foundation's history program director. The *News-Press* began profiling blues greats, among them Falls Church native John Jackson. "First Generation 'Piedmont Blues' Singer and 'the Greatest Finger-Picking Guitar Player in the World,'" said the paper's April 1999 write-up. Jackson's last concert was held on December 31, 2001, for the Falls Church Watch Night. The Virginia General Assembly's proclamation honoring him was reprinted in the *News-Press*.

Another Falls Church native got a write-up in February 2003: blues singer and harmonica virtuoso Little Sonny Warner, who had a gold record in 1959 titled "There's Something on Your Mind." The music festival opened a regular series of summer concerts sponsored by the Village Preservation and Improvement Society and the Friends of Cherry Hill Foundation. They've featured talents such as Deanna Bogart, descendants of Bob Marley's Wailers, Koko Taylor and Beatles tribute bands.

By the turn of the twenty-first century, the State Theatre was firing on all cylinders (eventually expanding from concerts to also hosting private corporate events and school reunions). Its vintage stage was graced by Jimmy Buffett in September 1999 (a surprise appearance that drew a crowd of four hundred), Pete Seeger in December 1999, Gregg Allman in February 2003 and Jimmy Cliff in March 2005. Over the years, the old movie theater marquee heralded concerts by Don McLean, Leon Russell, Peter Green, Jefferson Starship, Kinky Friedman, Warren Zevon, Dave Mason, Seldom Scene, the Amazing Rhythm Aces, John Mayall, Hanson and tribute bands for Bruce Springsteen, the Rolling Stones, the Doors and Queen. A favorite in recent years has been the 1980s-flavor dance band the Legwarmers, plus hat-loving guitarist Tom Principato and the Washington, D.C. R&B phenom the Nighthawks.

The *News-Press*'s concert coverage often took the form of "Press Pass" features by Drew Costley, Mike Hume, Leslie Poster or Matt Delaney. When the Nighthawks played at Alexandria's Birchmere in June 2015, Costley wrote like an insider. "Mark Wenner and his three bandmates in the roots music quartet The Nighthawks are stripping it down, going acoustic for their new album *Back Porch Party*, which was released in late April, and taking the party on the road," he reported. "The last time The Nighthawks made an acoustic album it was their first, 2011's *Last Train to Bluesville*, for which they won their first Blues Music Award."

When comedian and Aflack commercial duck voice actor Gilbert Gottfried appeared at the State Theatre in December 2019, Delaney scored an interview, writing: "Whether you know him from his days as a young stand-up comedian in New York City in the 1970s, as Iago from Disney's *Aladdin* or even one of his many raunchy sets for celebrity roasts, Gottfried is one of those Hollywood characters who finds a way to stick with you no matter how long he occupies the stage or screen."

It was also at the turn of the century that a jazz venue opened on West Broad Street. The Bangkok Steakhouse (later Bangkok Blues) is "fast becoming a prime live-music nightspot," the paper reported. In June 2002, the paper ran a photograph of banjo player and bluegrass composer Randy Barrett, a Falls Churchian, at Bangkok, and in September 2003, it featured the club's owner, Chai Siribongkot, jamming with a guitar for a "Save the Blues" benefit.

The folk scene in Falls Church is embodied by the Irish American musicians who perform at Ireland's Four Provinces and on the decades-beloved radio show *Traditions*, hosted by resident Mary Cliff. The Arlington-born veteran broadcaster at WAMU, WETA and the local WERA stations was profiled in May 2015 by Patricia Leslie. Cliff described her archive of music and reel-to-reel tapes of the interviews she's done with Pete Seeger, Mike Seeger, Arlo

Guthrie, Tom Paxton, the Nitty Gritty Dirt Band, Mary Chapin Carpenter and Garrison Keillor. "Her niche is folk music, which she says embraces all 'culturally related musics' including blues, classical, contemporary, which find their roots in folk, 'if you go back far enough.'"

The *News-Press* did not neglect the classical genre. In April 1992, Benton introduced readers to the Arlington Symphony's music director Ruben Vartanyan, a Russian Bolshoi defector. In April 1997, the paper reviewed that orchestra's performance of *A Glorious Verdi Requiem*. In July 1992, it interviewed opera singer Luciano Pavarotti at National Airport. A profile of Arlington-based opera singer Carl Tanner appeared in November 2004, and in April 2007, readers read about the poet James Ogelthorpe narrating the New Dominion Chorale performance of Schumann's *Quest for Paradise*.

Commentary on national television shows also crept in. Benton weighed in on the "vote 'em off the island" show *Survivor* in August 2000, favoring "airhead blond surfer" Greg as "the loser." And in September 2000, a *News-Press* feature was titled "Wild Kingdom's Jim Fowler Returns to Childhood Home in Falls Church." When an intriguing spy show debuted in 2017, the *News-Press* ran a feature: "One of the hottest shows on television today, *The Americans*, has a distinct connection to the city of Falls Church. Set in the 1980s during the Reagan era, the drama follows the lives and intrigues of KGB spies Philip and Elizabeth Jennings, whom 'the center' placed in Falls Church so they had access to Washington, D.C., and the government secrets they were tasked with discovering."

But to get the most bang for his buck from staff and freelancers, Benton branched out to review area concerts. In June 1999, he wrote up Judy Collins's show at Wolf Trap Farm Park in Vienna (her twenty-second at the outdoor amphitheater), and in August 2000, he reviewed Jethro Tull's show there. Reinforcing his baby boomer bias, in December 2005, Benton wrote an essay praising the career of Tina Turner as she received a Kennedy Center honor. And that venue's production of *Phantom of the Opera* merited a praising editorial in December 1993.

A poignant editorial on music in the July 9, 1998 issue, titled "The Message in the Music," was prompted by an appearance of Robert Plant and Jimmy Page at the downtown MCI Center. Benton expanded on his love for '60s and '70s music, writing about Plant's and Page's former band Led Zeppelin, Bob Dylan, the Rolling Stones, the Eagles and Van Morrison. Benton's December 2003 review of a Simon and Garfunkel concert at the MCI Center said, "Their works combine just the right mix of surface cynicism and inner hurt." Letters praising that review followed for weeks.

In May 2005, Benton used a quick feature "The Editor Recommends" to steer readers to a State Theatre appearance of the Grateful Dead cover band Dark Star Orchestra, with former Allman Brother Dickey Betts. (Benton would join younger staffers in selecting and printing a list of their generation's best songs in a given week.) A *News-Press* interview with Deejay Nic Harcourt by Mike Hume drew praise from reader Marilyn Terrell for being "better than the *Washington Post*."

Live community theater depends on local news to build a following. Falls Church is fortunate to have two troupes, the Providence Players of Fairfax and Creative Cauldron. The volunteer-run Players, after organizing in 2004, lobbied Fairfax County for use of the auditorium stage in the James Lee Community Center (just outside the Little City in a former all-Black school on Annandale Road named for a nineteenth-century Black landowner). In May 2005, *News-Press* reporter Darien Bates commented on the Players' women performers who countered the stereotype of women being competitive and overly dramatic. It went on to revive such classics as *The Front Page* and *You Can't Take It with You*, and modernize others, like *Cabaret Takes a Holiday*. Its 2021 original one-act *Boredom, Fear and Wine* captured the misery of life locked down by the pandemic. It was delivered via video stream (following an earlier production in the outdoor parking lot of the Italian Café). And its autumn 2022 production of David Mamet's 2008 Oval Office political satire *November*, featuring a guest appearance by Congressman Gerry Connolly, staged a prescient portrait of a president not unlike Donald Trump.

The more avant-garde company and education nonprofit Creative Cauldron, launched in 2002 (with some help from Benton) by Producing Director Laura Connors Hull, has enjoyed a discounted performance space at the ArtSpace Falls Church on South Maple Street. Beginning in 2023, it will enjoy negotiated space at the new Insight mixed-use complex that was built around the Whole Foods outlet at Washington and Broad Streets. Its original works include fresh adaptations of *Aesop's Fables* and a world premiere musical, *Ichabod: The Legend of Sleepy Hollow*.

Benton and the Creative Cauldron staff regularly review area high school productions of classics such as *Hello, Dolly!*, *Guys and Dolls*, *The Crucible* and *Urinetown*. The editor reviewed the Arena Stage productions of *Nicholas Nickleby*, *A Streetcar Named Desire* and Eleanor Roosevelt as portrayed by Jean Stapleton. In September 2003, he profiled eleven-year-old Falls Church resident actor Miles Butler, who performed downtown in Ford Theatre's production of *The Grapes of Wrath*.

Once the *News-Press* expanded to include mainstream movie advertising and nationally syndicated reviews by Roger Ebert, Benton often commented on new releases. His January 9, 1992 editorial deconstructed the Oliver Stone assassination conspiracy movie *JFK*, endorsing challenges to the famous Warren Report's conclusion that shooter Lee Harvey Oswald, on November 22, 1963, acted alone. The 1993 sexually avant-garde film *The Crying Game* was welcomed as being brave in a Benton editorial. His February 1997 essay on the film *Schindler's List* drew a letter of thanks from Jack Valenti, the president of the Motion Picture Association of America, saying it "was both literate and insightful." In February 2000, Benton found the Leo DeCaprio film *The Beach* to be "compelling," and in 2001, he nominated *Billy Elliot* for "Best Film of the Year."

Visual arts abound in the Little City. The Falls Church Art Gallery at 700 West Broad Street, in June 2019, mounted an *About Me* art show, showcasing seventy-one works in photography—oil and acrylic paintings, watercolors and mixed media and lithograph pieces. And in December 2022, the gallery staged *Bits and Pieces*, a "collection, or collage" of seemingly sad-eyed paintings, wrote reviewer *News-Press* reviewer Mark Dreisonstok. The

Benton communing with Motion Picture Association of America president Jack Valenti at the White House Correspondents' Dinner. *From the* News-Press.

exhibit, according to Dreisonstok, "would seem to disprove the quote widely attributed to Austrian poet Rainer Maria Rilke that 'shattered people are best represented by bits and pieces.'" The exhibit, he added, "can represent, in the words of one artist, a 'search for balance and rhythm,' both for the artist and the viewer."

Published books of local interest drew steady *News-Press* ink. In July 1995, readers learned that murder mystery author Wade B. Fleetwood had published "A Beach Reunion in Falls Church, Virginia." And in May 2005, the paper profiled Falls Church–based freelance journalist Jeff Bagato for his *Mondo D.C.: An Insider's Guide to Washington D.C's Unusual Tourist Attractions.*

Openings for fun venues were faithfully chronicled. July 1997 brought the debut of what became a popular mini-golf course at Jefferson Park on Lee Highway. When the Bowl America lanes, a fixture on South Maple Street since 1960, got a makeover in August 2016, the *News-Press* was on the case. "There is an array of bowling lane machinery set about the outside the building and skeletal structures of the lanes are exposed," said the photograph's caption. (Bowl America got a new lease on life when the national chain Bowlero bought it in 2021.)

The Little City's prime toy store, the Doodlehopper, was welcomed on West Broad Street in September 2002. And in a most unusual happening, the paper, in May 2003, announced its first annual Wacky Hat Show at the coming Memorial Day festival. First prize would win a fifty-dollar restaurant coupon.

Though it's hardly unbiased in this case, the *News-Press*, for decades, provided regular photographic coverage of its annual holiday parties. In total, 160 guests attended the December 1992 gala (eight photographs were published), and in December 1993, the headline read, "[Congressman Jim Moran] Hails NP Holiday Party as New Falls Church Tradition." The more boastful title for the December 2006 edition read, "N-P Holiday Party Once Again Featured A-List Celebs Among 200."

14

Doing Good

F alls Churchians who look beyond themselves donate treasure and time to the poorly funded, the poorly housed and the poorly treated components of our good Earth. The *News-Press* has both covered and participated in such charity. "Falls Church is an exceptional community for the warmth of its citizens and the support and recognition provided for those engaged in volunteer work," wrote Benton in a June 1993 editorial on "Avoiding Burnout." Prompted by a shortage of candidates willing to join advisory panels, he cited one reason: "jealous, petty criticism," an oblique reference to some resignations by volunteers protesting the appointment of others. Following a touching turnout of volunteers to pitch in for others following a blizzard in January 1996, one reader asked, "Do you realize there is a vast pool of talented people willing to service Falls Church but they are turned down because they live just over the city limits?"

In March 1991, there was an announcement that the taxpayer-supported Aurora House Girls Home at 420 South Maple Street had opened its doors to twelve residents between the ages of thirteen and seventeen under Juvenile Treatment Services. Some in the Falls Church Citizens Organization had opposed its funding, calling it a "prison." By April 1997, auction house executive Paul Quinn was helping raise money for a Susan B. Olom Scholarship Fund to help Aurora House residents, ultimately delivering $15,000. Similarly, the *News-Press* reported in July 2005 that the city had dedicated the Miller House, a shelter for transitioning single women and their children at 366 North Washington Street, which had been in the city's hands since 1973. In

Left: The George Mason monument was erected at city hall in 1999 to honor volunteers. Twenty-two years later, Mason's name came off the city high school. *Author's photograph.*

Below: Falls Churchians of all ages assemble to do their part in easing food insecurity. *From the* News-Press.

October 2017, the city council voted to transfer the group home to community residences with a sale price of $1 and $300,000 from the Virginia Department of Behavioral Health and Development Services.

Beginning in May 1993, the newspaper joined with the chamber of commerce in an annual food drive, with bags for donated goods getting distributed inside copies of the paper. The paper's coverage also highlighted Falls Churchians who aided the Washington, D.C. Central Kitchen food bank. May 2006 brought coverage of the first "Elementary PTA-sponsored Home and Garden Tour," which drew three hundred participants and was organized by one hundred volunteers who raised $9,800 to enhance the public schools. After Hurricane Katrina flooded Louisiana and Mississippi in August 2005, the city council voted to donate $10,000 to the Red Cross. And when a deadly tsunami hit Asia in December 2005, George Mason students put on a bake sale that raised $29,000 for victims.

More personalized efforts showed. In November 2002, students and parents held a gala to raise money for Abigail's Alliance, a charity formed in honor of Abigail Burroughs, a George Mason alumna from the class of '98 who died of cancer in June 2001 while at the University of Virginia. Two years later, young people set up lemonade stands led by pediatric cancer victim Carolyn Coveney, age five, and her parents, helping raise $1 million.

Congressman Jim Moran, in May 1996, led a VIP walk to benefit a local child development center. June 1997 brought *News-Press*'s photographic coverage under the headline "AIDS Riders to Traverse Falls Church," in which a team, including Benton, biked 350 miles from Raleigh, North Carolina, to Washington, D.C., to raise $4 million for Whitman Walker Clinic, which specializes in AIDS treatment. "A Chronicle of the Great AIDS Ride" included day-by-day coverage and a photograph of Benton on his bike. The *News-Press*'s Danny O'Brien joined a separate three-day bike ride from Boston to New York that attracted 3,188 riders and raised $7 million in memory of Falls Church banker Bob Blanchard, who died from AIDS.

Benton and the newspaper's staff, in March 1988, helped local public TV-radio station WETA by manning its pledge drive phones. A photograph of the gang with famed singer Sarah Brightman was later published. A few charitable acts rose in unexpected circumstances. "Baby Born on Bike Trail," read the paper's grabby headline in May 1997. The story delivered details of the surprise outdoor experience of Catherine and Steve Schmitt, who were forced to bring their third child into the world while hiking the W&OD bike trail near Spring Street. Luckily, passerby Beatrice Brady was a nurse. Steve cut the umbilical cord outdoors and welcomed his baby girl.

In March 2001, a wayward car crashed into the Aladdin's Lamp Bookstore on West Broad Street. The *News-Press*'s caption described proprietor Alina Gawlik as "still in business, but could use more!"

For a decade before the Whittier site was redeveloped, the organized food bank for Falls Church was Lazarus at the Gate. In January 1994, the *News-Press* editorial pleaded with the city to "Keep Lazarus," but the next month, the food bank was "Forcibly Evicted from Whittier as Winter Storm Rages." Lazarus director George McManmon thanked the paper for its support, as did accountant Mike Diener. The food bank moved to Merrifield, where it continues as Food for Others Inc.

Another clash arose around the Unity Club, a meeting place for members of Alcoholics Anonymous and other recovery fellowships at 116 B West Broad Street. Supporter Diener called the facility "one of the nation's best 12-step programs." In 1995, the city decided not to renew the club's parking permit, with some council members hinting at a view that it was "bringing in the wrong kind of people," as Diener recalled. Suddenly, users found their cars being towed. But the club brings in $2.7 million to the city with hundreds of visitors per week, and the issue resurfaced in 1999. The *News-Press* published advertisements listing businesses and individuals who donate to the club, which endures.

Education is an area where the newspaper also put its money where its reporting was. The June 19, 2003 issue carried a photograph of Mason High student and *News-Press* employee Drew Maier with Benton as the recipient of a *News-Press* college scholarship. In April 2004, citizen activists Dick McCall, Kieran Sharpe and Bob Young petitioned the city council for $50,000 to add to the seed money they came up with to launch the Falls Church Education Foundation. (Benton kicked in an additional $15,000 in April 2005 and added his own subunit to encourage an affirmation for diversity in student life.)

The foundation, run in recent years by executive director (and city councilwoman) Debbie Hiscott, solicits donations and holds auctions to fund college scholarships and grants for staff training in all five city schools.

The Little City's push-and-pull efforts to aid the homeless is often a political football. Carol Jackson, who ran the city's homelessness programs in both charity and housing policy, recalled how her early efforts to launch a winter shelter drew resistance. "Many Falls Churchians didn't want to share with people who don't look like them, which made me mad," she recalled in 2022. The only place the shelter was allowed to operate was an industrial zone near Route 7 and the old railroad tracks. That first year, she remembered having to bus the clients to the Bailey's Shelter & Supportive Housing facility in nearby Fairfax, "before the sun came up so that no one could see 12 homeless men coming in and out of our pristine community." In January 1996, the *News-Press* reported on a new ordinance that allowed the shelter to use a site near Don Beyer Volvo as the emergency winter shelter. And Farouq Massoud of the Washington Flyer transport service agreed to allow temporary use of his facility at 1115 West Broad Street. The city then offered the warehouse it owned at 217 Gordon Road to provide both shelter and counseling to the needy, and it still operates. A smattering of help came in January 1998, with donations from a *News-Press*-sponsored three-on-three basketball tournament, with entry fees to benefit the homeless.

That same month, the Hollywood producers of the hit show *The X-Files* donated $150 to the cause in return for the use of an image of a Falls Church police car. "Falls Church Needs a Year-Round Homeless Shelter," argued Teman Treadway in a letter to the editor. Some library patrons complained about the homeless loitering in the reading room. In January 2006, a front-page story reported that "Falls Church Homeless Shelters Feel Regional Trend Is Shortage of Beds and Resources for the Homeless." By the year's end, the City Health Department had issued new restrictions, saying the Gordon Street shelter needed an operating license for vendors.

With Falls Church's reputation of being Tree City, as determined by the National Arbor Day Foundation, its earnest volunteers strive to live up to the billing. The green movement has been strong enough that the city newsletter gives regular tips on recycling, and locals mark Earth Day with plantings. When Cherry Hill Park was targeted by some for development in 1999, citizens rallied with a coalition to "Save Our Park from Politics." The federal Environmental Protection Agency, in January 1998, said Falls Church had the "highest diversion rate" (the percentage of recycled material not incinerated or put in landfills) of all localities surveyed. And in January 2000, the EPA named the city number 1 in waste reduction.

Judith Lemke, the chair of the Recycling and Litter Prevention Council (founded in 1989 and, in 2003, absorbed into the broader Environmental Services Council), wrote to the *News-Press* to correct citizen misinformation on fees and collection stickers. In January 2005, city arborist Jill-Anne Spence was recognized by the International Society of Arboriculture. And in November 2010, the Virginia Department of Environmental Quality ranked Falls Church first out of 324 localities in recycling.

By the twenty-first century, the city was encouraging its citizens to recycle discarded computers and other electronics, designating special days for

Village Preservation and Improvement Society activists Robert Tartt and Keith Thurston boost history at the farmers' market. *Author's photograph.*

this and partnering with the private firm eAsset Solutions, which the *News-Press* profiled in May 2021. Operating out of the former Quinn Auction Warehouse on North Maple Street, eAsset Solutions receives discarded goods from individuals and contracts with large employers that toss out dated equipment during upgrades. Technicians perform privacy law–required data destruction using environmentally sustainable techniques.

The headline for Arbor Day in April 2000, however, was "City Trees Disappearing." A commission finding had prompted mobilization by the Village Preservation and Improvement Society, which, in addition to its home design and garden awards, runs a Neighborhood Tree Program to protect the tree canopy.

In May 2001, the *News-Press* ran a photograph of costumed environmentalists in Frady Park reenacting Falls Church's first Arbor Day back in 1892. Their tree planting honored civic activists Roger Wollenberg and deceased former school board member Yvette Eldridge. And in 2004, the city plan incorporated a ten-year program to protect the town's canopy. The value of tree preservation is not universal. In an April 27, 2000 letter, reader Dennis Tolliver cited George Mason's concept of property rights in arguing that for landowners who needed to cut them, "trees are private property."

15

GAY IN FALLS CHURCH

S ociety's shift toward the acceptance of homosexuality evolved through rapid cultural changes in the three decades that were covered by the *News-Press*, which itself evolved on the emphasis it gave the subject. Though editor Benton came out while in graduate school in the early 1970s, the newspaper devoted far more space to development, schools and holiday celebrations than the fluid debate over the gay community.

In the 1990s and into the twenty-first century, many individuals and religious groups disapproved of gay sex and same-sex marriage. "It is criminal conduct for schoolteachers to teach about homosexuality in a positive light," wrote reader Marion Lelong in August 1994. She was responding to a Benton editorial criticizing the U.S. Senate for withholding funds from schools that address the issue.

And when the Presbyterian Church, in 2001, announced its acceptance of same-sex marriage, a March 21 letter from K.C. McAlpin protested that "Presbyterian moral standards are not meant to change every 20–30 years." During the 2003 fight over Falls Church Episcopal's plan to close a street for its expansion, reader Danie M. Gray blasted the *News-Press* editorial for attacking "treasured tenets of faith....There would not even be a City of Falls Church which could pass its morally relativistic ordinances on sexual preferences without the Falls Church." And Democratic state delegate Jim Scott, in October 2001, announced that he personally opposed gay marriage.

But things changed after the October 1998 murder of a twenty-two-year-old gay man named Matthew Shepard in rural Wyoming. Benton dramatized the incident in an editorial headlined "Hate Crime." And in April 1999, the city council passed a "No Hate Here" resolution that welcomed diversity, "regardless of their race, color, religion, sex, sexual orientation, pregnancy, national origin, age, marital status or disability."

The reaction was not necessarily partisan—Delegate Bob Hull's Republican opponent in 2001 was Danny Smith, who was openly gay. After the terrorist attacks of September 11, Benton's editorial slammed conservative Virginia preachers Jerry Fallwell and Pat Robertson for blaming the murders on Americans' tolerance of abortion and the gay community. (The two later conceded their remarks were ill-timed.)

Momentum toward acceptance continued. When high school drama teacher Frank Marino was arrested for having sex with an underage teen, the *News-Press* published a letter from nine-year-old Genevieve Jordan defending gay marriage. In October 2002, the *News-Press* announced it would begin printing marriage notices for same-sex unions (following the *Roanoke Times* and 139 other papers). The previous April, Benton published his interview with Representative Barney Frank, who had come out as gay in 1989, conducted at the Jefferson-Jackson Day potluck.

In June 2003, the *News-Press* endorsed Adam Ebbin, who became the first openly gay Virginia delegate, in the Democratic primary. And Benton ran a photograph of himself at the dinner of the gay-oriented Human Rights Campaign with gay Episcopal bishop Gene Robinson in October 2004. At that dinner the following year, Benton was photographed with Frank Kameny, the pioneer in the effort to end government persecution of homosexuals going back to the 1950s. (Benton would later write a Kameny profile, host him in a discussion and publish a photograph of him in 2006, when Kameny visited Falls Church after donating his papers to the Library of Congress.) A *News-Press* editorial from February 26, 2004, blasted the George W. Bush administration's support of banning gay marriage and called for civil disobedience. And Benton's editorial in July 2005 was titled "Hail the U.C.C." after the United Church of Christ's Atlanta Synod backed marriage equality.

It was around that time that *News-Press* readers were introduced to the columns of gay activist Wayne Besen, which were titled "Anything but Straight." In a June 2004 essay, Besen criticized former president Ronald Reagan, who had just died, for his record of slow-walking research into the causes of AIDS in the 1980s, calling the policy a "gash on the face of the Mona Lisa." "Thank you for publishing Wayne Besen's eloquent, moving piece," said a letter from Jo Miller in December 2004. "I am proud of the

In 2005, gay rights pioneer Frank Kameny posed with then–vice president Joe Biden and Benton at a White House LGBTQ event in 2009. *From the* News-Press.

FCNP." But Besen's charge that evangelical pastor and author Rick Warren "lacked love" in dealing with gays drew a rebuttal from Richard Foley of Saddleback Church, published on December 15, 2005.

By 2006, Benton was more open in his coverage of the gay community. He reprinted an account of the New York City "Empress Ball" from the gay magazine *Scene*. He used his own column to blast Jerry Falwell for being "hell-bent" on pushing programs to convert gay people into straight people. And his review of a concert by Madonna, who promoted AIDS relief early on, described her as a threat to homophobes, as she was a "smart, political woman." Benton was accused of hypocrisy, however, for his negative take on Republican congressman Mark Foley's exposure for having pressed male congressional pages for sex. Reader Peter Byrd, in a letter in the August 11, 2005 issue, charged that Benton had provided more sympathetic coverage of high school drama teacher Frank Marino, who was arrested for sex with an underage teen. A June 2005 letter from George Hale accused the *News-Press* of "blind devotion to the gay agenda" and making "an absolute mockery of balanced journalism." In an editor's note, Benton replied, "It's not about any gay agenda other than equal rights."

A big issue during the mid-2000s was the nation's conservative government's efforts to bolster traditional marriage. In 2004, the Virginia General Assembly passed an "Affirmation of Marriage Act," banning civil unions and same-sex marriage—over the objections of Democratic governor Mark Warner. In 2006, the U.S. Senate, prompted by President Bush's campaign promises, considered "The Federal Marriage Amendment" to the Constitution to legally define marriage as being between one man and one woman. It fell just short. But the Virginia legislature succeeded in getting a statewide ballot referendum on a marriage amendment. "Will Virginia Be the First?" asked Benton in a May 25, 2006 editorial opposing the referendum. He argued the marriage amendment "makes gay sex seem disgusting." A news story in October quoted the CEO of Qorvis Communications as saying the amendment will hurt competitiveness. A subsequent letter from Sharon Depoorter called the marriage article "inaccurate" and based on "scare tactics." The headline in the November 9 issue read, "Marriage Amendment Passes, but May Have Cost [Republican Senator George] Allen the Election." That December, activist Gerald Filbin asked the Falls Church City Council to urge a repeal of Virginia's Affirmation of Marriage Act (an effort ongoing in 2023). "Thanks to you and your staff for being such a profound voice here in Falls Church," read a letter from Randy Butler in the January 18, 2007 issue. The *News-Press* is "a local paper that matched our political and personal beliefs. Keep fighting the good fight." By that November, the *News-Press*'s circulation of 36,500 matched that of the *Washington Blade* for the gay community. Benton made an unsuccessful attempt to buy the other weekly.

Benton proceeded to publish, from October 15, 2010, to September 7, 2012, one hundred columns titled "Nick Benton's Gay Science." Reprinted in the Washington, D.C.–based *Metro Weekly*, his essays challenged contemporary assumptions by citing the work of literary giants Oscar Wilde, Christopher Isherwood and Tennessee Williams. "Contrary to the shallow conceits of current, hedonistic urban gay culture, we gay souls have been a major, constructive factor in civilization since before the beginning," Benton wrote. "Sensitive to the plight of women, children, the elderly and downtrodden in savage patriarchal male chauvinist, war-mongering cultures, we worked to build the institutions over eons that have advanced compassion over cruelty, science over superstition, beauty over corruptions and equality over tyranny."

The gay science essays were published in 2013 by Lethe Press under the title *Extraordinary Hearts* and earned a praising review by gay pioneer and icon Larry Kramer. Benton followed it up with *Education of a Gay Soul*, published in 2021 by Benton Communications. In a June 19, 1922 editorial, he effused about being introduced during Gay Pride Week at the annual "Cappies" Theater Awards at the Kennedy Center. Amid the "loudest and most thunderous applause ever heard in my life," Benton reflected with gratitude that, "as one whose LGBTQ+ rights pioneering efforts go back 50 years, it was right for me to step up like this in such an unscripted situation."

Benton began to combine the increasingly visible gay issues with the paper's broader advocacy agenda. "As the City of Falls Church fights its own battles to emerge as a fiscally viable entity with long-term sustainability achieved through fresh economic development initiatives, it is essential that it become famous for a welcoming and affirming disposition toward racial, sexual, gender and lifestyle diversity," he wrote in a February 2, 2007 editorial headlined "The Real Falls Church." "The world needs to know that this is who we truly are."

16

Columns and Features

I nsight, advocacy, personality and lighthearted escapes. All are traits of a good newspaper's columns and entertainment features.

The *News-Press* was fortunate to tap area office holders (who wrote for free), reliable local essayists and sophisticated national bylines Benton accessed through inexpensive syndication. A sizable portion of the Falls Church readership, though interested in national and international affairs, would not be paid subscribers to the *New York Times*. So, they appreciated a weekly dose of Thomas Friedman, Paul Krugman, Maureen Dowd, David Brooks and William Safire.

But Benton's conduit to such star talent would also draw brickbats. In the late 1990s, the *News-Press* began reprinting the Hearst-syndicated column of Helen Thomas, the "doyenne" of White House correspondents whose career in the limelight with UPI went back to the Kennedy administration. Benton was a fan. He covered her being honored at the April 1998 White House Correspondents' Dinner. That January, he wrote an editorial, "The Governor and Helen Thomas," describing Thomas's reflections on her thirty-eight years covering presidents. He paired his commentary with a column by new Republican Virginia governor Jim Gilmore, whose debut that week discussed his state's 12 percent economic growth and his plans to take advantage of a government surplus. "People Can Handle the Truth and Deserve No Less" was the headline on Benton's coverage of Thomas's November 1999 speech on Presidents Clinton and Carter to Leadership Fairfax.

Under the George W. Bush administration, with war clouds gathering over Iraq, Thomas blasted Bush for launching a war based on fear of weapons of mass destruction that were never found. Benton's White House column defended Thomas against right-wing critics. In a January 22, 2004 interview with *Vanity Fair*, Thomas called Bush "the worst president in American history." That July, after a preview in the *News-Press*, the headline read, "Helen Thomas Makes Historic Visit to FC as Guest of *News-Press*." She drew 150 attendees at a small church sanctuary. Alongside text and photographs was Benton's editorial: "The Incomparable Helen Thomas." But reader M.F. Johnson, the following February, sent a scolding letter, "The *FCNP* can do better than Helen Thomas," citing "holes and inconsistencies" in her columns.

Thomas spoke again in Falls Church in December 2005 about "soul-searching" by the news media, having warned that Bush's selection of Judge Samuel Alito for the Supreme Court would put "abortion and civil rights in jeopardy." In July 2006, her new book *Watchdogs of Democracy* merited a full-page advertisement in the *News-Press*, and she attended a summer staff party.

But Thomas, a Lebanese Arab American, ran into trouble in June 2010. At an Obama White House celebration of Jewish heritage, she was filmed telling a rabbi that "[the Jews] should get the hell out of Palestine" and "go home" to Poland, Germany and the United States. The reaction from most quarters was furious, including pushback from the president's spokesman, as critics called her unfair to Israel. Thomas apologized and resigned from Hearst. Who would take her on at the age of eighty-nine? Benton contended that her comments were taken out of context and that she was not anti-Semitic. So, Thomas's final year in her career—her last before her death in 2013—was as a columnist for the *Falls Church News-Press*. (The hire, however, prompted advertising salesman Joe Friedling, who was Jewish, to quit.)

One of Benton's homegrown nationally noted columnists was Tom Whipple. His "Peak Oil" series, launched in April 2005, took advantage of his thirty-five years at the CIA. (Whipple had a second career compiling a daily clip service of Virginia political news.) He first wrote a sixteen-part series before converting it to a regular column that lasted for more than a decade. Whipple warned that fossil fuel is running out. He argued early for electric cars for the post office and warned, "It's time to start planning." In December 2006, he asked, "Is the Energy Information Administration 'the greatest failure of them all?' Instead, 'Peak Oil' should rank up there as one of the most important problems Congress should be looking at," he wrote in the

Legendary White House reporter-columnist Helen Thomas fields questions from CNN in the *News-Press* office soon after Benton hired her 2011. *From the* News-Press.

November 30, 2006 edition. The *Washington Post* (and, later, the *New York Times*), he wrote that July, was ignoring the possibility of imminent peak oil. Thanks to internet distribution, fan mail poured in from around the country. "Peak Oil" was "a wake-up call," wrote reader Doug Goodgion in August 2006. "Wish we had a newspaper like yours in Charlotte," wrote North Carolinian Steve Voetsch. But skeptics weighed in, too. "'Peak Oil' is just another scam," said a letter from William Forrestal (via the internet) in July 2005. The *News-Press*'s April 26, 2007 edition carried a photograph of Whipple lecturing ex–Virginia governor (and later senator) Mark Warner.

Tom Whipple's columns often appeared in the same issues as columns by his wife, Mary Margaret Whipple. A one-time Arlington School Board and County Board member who was elected to the Virginia State Senate, she wrote columns on Richmond goings on, such as the creation of a monument for notable Virginia women and housing and healthcare issues. When Ms. Whipple arrived as a senator-elect in January 2009, her *News-Press* column described the transitions in Washington and the Virginia capital. "In my capacity as chair of the Environment Committee of the National Conference of State Legislatures, I was invited to meet with the transition agency review team at the Environmental Protection Agency," she wrote. "They had

Arlington-based state senator Mary Margaret Whipple and "Peak Oil" columnist Tom Whipple made a Falls Church power couple. *From the* News-Press.

thoughtful questions about the agency's relationships with states and how they can be improved. I was impressed with their attention to process as well as substance." In October 2021, the *News-Press* covered a reception honoring both Whipples, attended by prominent Democrats.

Neighboring Arlington is of interest to Falls Churchians. So, Benton named Richard Barton to write the "Our Man in Arlington" weekly column. A jovial community activist and academic, Barton wrote movingly on the sudden death of newly installed county board chairman Charles Monroe in January 2003, as well as the tragic death of U.S. senator Paul Wellstone (D-MN), a graduate of Arlington's Yorktown High School, in a plane crash in October 2002. As a declared Democrat, Barton wrote often of the party's annual Labor Day chili cookoff and of the gadflies who haunt the county board on its New Year's Day meeting. He also speculated on the identity of the mysterious author who wrote a novel on Arlington politics under the name Jane Barcroft.

In 2010, Barton was replaced by Charlie Clark, the author of this volume. His "Our Man in Arlington" column took a reporter's neutral approach, quoting both sides on issues and providing more on-scene coverage. In addition to covering politics and policy, the new Arlington column featured history, famous Arlingtonians, neighborhood life and humor. Grateful for the reader praise, Clark went on to publish books and emerged as a public speaker.

As the World Wide Web arrived, managing editor Jody Fellows, in February 2006, launched a column highlighting useful things he'd found on the internet. Benton also made use of paid staff by dispatching Fellows, Darien Bates and Peter Laub to review restaurants in the greater Falls Church area.

High school teacher Mike Hoover's column tapped his insider status to give readers a glimpse into education, combined with his cultural interests. "Computers Now in all City Classrooms," he wrote in August 1996. He examined school rankings in January 1998 and plagiarism and the George Mason High School honor code in January 2002. Benton allowed Hoover to weigh in on such topics as the 1997 death of comedian Bill Cosby's son Ennis and the "match of the century" chess tournament that year between Russian Garry Kasparov and the IBM Deep Blue computer. When Hoover retired after thirty-seven years in June 2007, he was the Mason High graduation speaker, and Benton gave him a full-page send-off.

Among the earliest of politicos to write for the *News-Press* was state Delegate Bob Hull. His January 1993 column revealed the reasoning behind his decision to replace the predictable title "Richmond Report" with "Coffin Corner," a reference to where he sat in the General Assembly's hallway. In July, Hull wrote on new laws taking effect. "Spreading the Surplus Made it a Good Year in Richmond," Hull reported in March 1999. He also contributed features, including an August 2006 piece on Virginia's "Crooked Road" country music history trail.

The longest serving of Benton's columnists was Penny Gross, the Fairfax supervisor regularly reelected to represent the Bailey's Crossroads area. She wrote on practical issues—where to donate blood, the call for speed bumps on certain roads and snow removal arrangements. In January 2004, she celebrated the history of Lake Barcroft, and she has been influential in revitalizing Bailey's commercial base. She chose not to seek reelection in 2023.

Of the U.S. congressmen, Democrat Jim Moran (who served from 1991 to 2015) appeared for the longest stretch in the *News-Press*, with columns on federal appropriations affecting the region. He mixed commentary on the presidency with discussions of governing's nuts and bolts. "I plan to introduce legislation in the coming weeks to create a regional, $20 million conservation program that would be administered by the National Park Service," Moran wrote in January 2009. "The Service's National Capital Region would solicit proposals by the two states, the District, the local governments and any nonprofits that propose to acquire or preserve land within the D.C. region and Potomac River watershed."

Moran's seat was virtually inherited by Don Beyer. He had written a *News-Press* column (including in its first edition) as Virginia's lieutenant governor and continued a sophisticated take on the economy, healthcare, women's issues and science. "Northern Virginia is one of the most intelligent, diverse, and engaged constituencies in our country," he wrote in January 2015. "The chance to represent such a district in Congress is a great honor, a great responsibility." In January 2021, during the pandemic, Beyer wrote that "every Virginian adult aged 16 and older is eligible to get a free Covid-19 vaccine. This vaccine will save your life." And as the Supreme Court prepared to overturn the half-century-old *Roe v. Wade* decision, Beyer, in January 2022, wrote of abortion as a key to economic freedom: "Access to abortion not only shapes the economic outcomes of the pregnant person, but also the economic circumstances that children grow up in."

Another traditional liberal *News-Press* columnist was Delegate Jim Scott, whose "Richmond Report," in 2006, provided behind-the-scenes updates on legislation affecting transportation, the estate tax and tax credits for land preservation. Benton appreciated Scott's shepherding of a House

Falls Church's "favorite son" and future Democratic congressman Don Beyer (*left*) chats with U.S. senator and former Virginia governor Chuck Robb. *From the* News-Press.

joint resolution, citing the *News-Press* for "advocating affordable housing, quality education, support for the disenfranchised, and human rights and equality…[being] one of the few general interest community newspapers in the nation to publish a weekly column dedicated to gay and lesbian justice issues." And as Benton wrote in a tribute after Scott died from Alzheimer's disease in April 2017, "When, in his opinion, we endorsed the wrong candidate once or when we made an off-handed deprecating comment about people in his birthplace in southwest Virginia, he did not hesitate to roast us."

Another longstanding political column was penned by state senator Dick Saslaw. "This year," he wrote in September 2019, "Virginia celebrates 400 years and the title of the longest continuously serving legislative body in the Americas. Legendary thinkers set up the democratic processes we still follow today. Our history richly fulfills the American dream sought by many and tested on numerous occasions in battle. It is also blemished with inequities we strive to right within our democratic boundaries." He retired in 2023.

Delegate Marcus Simon, who took over for Scott, wrote a Richmond Report in December 2022 that read, "As a member of leadership in the House Democratic Caucus (Deputy Floor Leader), I participated in a panel for the Virginia Press Association recently on the issue of Education and parental rights, where I was able to highlight the real issue behind recent headlines—a desire to undermine public education." The previous April, he lambasted new governor Glenn Youngkin for issuing more vetoes than his predecessors. "Youngkin vetoed 26 popular bi-partisan bills that passed with the support of the conservative Republican led House of Delegates and the Democratic-controlled State Senate."

The successor to Delegate Hull, who beat him in a primary in 2009, was Kaye Kory. For a dozen years, her column focused on police reform, gun safety and voting rights. "Imagine how many people in our Commonwealth could successfully register if we had a functioning voter registration system in place, as the Democratic majority envisioned when approving funds in 2021 for an update of the so-old-it-creaks system we have in place now," she wrote in November 2022. "We should stop the talk that undermines public confidence in elections and move our national conversation to substance." She stepped down in 2023.

To entertain and to liven layouts, the *News-Press* brought both original and syndicated visuals and short, stand-alone texts. The most popular original feature was the photograph-centered "Critter Corner." Executed initially by Simon van Steyn, with reader contributions beginning in 1994, the

"Critter Corner" might show you a Falls Church family pet named Lobby the hamster. Or it might announce, "Spooky's Back," detailing the story of a kitty being rescued by a Taco Bell worker after it was found dumped in the drive-through. A reader, in April 2002, sent a letter lauding "Critter Corner" for its "warmth, humor and charm." In April 1996, the Mary Riley Styles Library put on an exhibit of *News-Press* critters, using the bound volumes (and later PDFs) that Benton regularly donated. In January 1992, readers were shown exclusive editorial cartoons by Doug Graham that used the elephant and donkey to comment on national politics. After Graham mocked Clinton's victory that November, a letter from Bradley Strahan chided, "I have been disturbed by its right-wing editorial stance all along, but this last egregiously scurrilous cartoon by Mr. Graham is the final blow." Benton appended an editor's note, observing that the editorial cartoon is the artist's "own opinion." Later editorial cartoons were drawn by intern and webmaster Lucas Hardi.

Starting at the *News-Press* in 1997, local artist Mark Rowe and resident word-player Neil Shawen began publishing a visual titled "Puntoons," which applied puns to current topics. The feature later became a book.

Benton, beginning in 1997, personally contributed a hand-drawn *Nick Knack* cartoon weekly for two decades. This opportunity to display a creative side produced, for example, a gag published in the August 13, 1998 issue showing a snake charmer and two snakes, one saying, "I don't know about you, but I think he's charming." In October 1999, the drawing

Page 18--FALLS CHURCH NEWS-PRESS--Thursday, May 7, 1998

To purchase your own book(s) of *Puntoons!*, visit Brown's Hardware, 100 W. Broad St.

The *News-Press* showcased the drawings by local artist Mark Rowe and resident word player Neil Shawen. *Author's photograph.*

showed two sheep, with one declaring, "I understand that Georgetown has a great *baaah* scene."

As a nurturer of talent, Benton published syndicated professional comic strips not found in competing papers. Beginning in 2004, readers were treated to *Loose Parts*, by Dave Blazek (later picked up by the *Washington Post*). Following on its heels from syndicates were the *The Quigmans*, by Buddy Hickerson; *Out on a Limb*, by Gary Kopervas; *Just Like Cats and Dogs*, by Dave T. Phipps; *Captain RibMan*, by John and Rich Davis; and *Wombania*, by Peter Marinacci.

When the *News-Press* turned ten, it qualified for a reprint column titled "Back in the Day: 5 and 10 Years Ago."

And last but, yes, *least*, the paper made layouts tidier with "filler" items, usually famous provocative quotations. "Be kind, for everyone you meet is fighting a harder battle than you," quoth Plato. They could be humorous headline bloopers from the Virginia Press Association: "Milk Drinkers Are Turning to Powder." They could be self-serving: "Tell 'em You Saw It in the *News-Press*." Or they could be Benton's favorite from Shakespeare: "To thine own self be true."

17

NATIONAL AND WORLD NEWS BEATS

L ocal News, Global Perspective," became a *News-Press* slogan in late 2004. Consider the readership: Falls Church is populated by educated, well-traveled citizens, many of whom explored the world via jobs in the government or military. So, it made sense for even a local paper just outside the media-saturated capital to combine village intimacy with cosmopolite coverage of the region, the state, the federal government and dramas overseas. Editor Benton published analysis and political endorsements, and sure as night follows day, he drew criticism.

"You put out a first-rate local newspaper that provides a service to the community not duplicated by any other medium," read a letter from Connelly Stevenson, complaining of the September 1994 coverage of "bigger issues." (The paper had covered President Clinton's policy to help remove a dictator in poverty-stricken Haiti, and it included a photograph of Clinton's top officials William Perry, Warren Christopher and John Shalikashvili.) "Why not stick to your knitting?" Benton appended a reply: "We have been proud of the fact that, since our inception, as a newspaper serving a highly educated community inside the Beltway, we have been frequently blessed with outstanding reports and commentaries on matters of interest beyond our local community."

In the same month, on September 29, 1994, another headline read, "Disney Says It's Pulling Out of Haymarket Site." The paper announced that the long-discussed vision for an American history theme park on I-66, near Gainesville, Virginia, was a no-go. That bugged Benton, who, after interviewing and observing presentations by Disney staff, had editorialized in favor of the park, despite local worries about thickened traffic. His editorial described Disney's decision as a "great frustration and disappointment," the opposition coming from "wealthy interests, not history folks or property owners."

In one of its earliest issues, on March 28, 1991, the *News-Press* covered an appearance by former attorney general Elliot Richardson, who spoke on George Mason at the Bill of Rights Bicentennial Commemoration Dinner, sponsored by the Falls Church Commission on the Bicentennial and the Village Preservation and Improvement Society. In June 1997, Secretary of State Madeleine Albright was the graduation speaker at Mason High. "Can't Draw Lines of Indifference on a World Map," read the paper's headline, published with the full text. "She impressed everyone, stayed for the whole event," read Benton's editorial, alongside two pages of photographs, "restoring faith in the decency and honor of good people in public service."

An example of the commingling of the Little City and world affairs came in June 1998, when, with help from Benton's academic brother Stephen, the city and George Mason University teamed up for a gathering that was written up with the headline "Historic Information Technology Confab Draws 1700 from 93 nations to Area." The November 12, 1998 issue carried a photograph of military experts visiting the high school, as four-star general Jack Vesey had a granddaughter in school there. In November 2006, the paper covered former president Jimmy Carter's book signing at the Bailey's Crossroads Borders Bookstore. That volume, *Palestine: Peace Not Apartheid*, contained controversial analysis of America's involvement in the Middle East. And in August 2007, the paper ran photographs of Falls Church resident Pete Geren's swearing-in as secretary of the army.

Benton used outsiders and his own commentary and features to weigh in on nonlocal issues. "Why International Terrorism Hasn't Been a Factor in the Gulf War," read a September 1992 essay by consultant Mayer Nudell. After cult leader David Koresh led Branch Davidians to a fiery death outside Waco, Texas, in April 1993, Benton wrote editorials titled "Hell to Pay" and "Psychological Tyranny." When Johnson administration defense secretary Robert McNamara published a memoir, Benton's editorial noted his "dismal confession" that the Vietnam was "one big mistake."

Many of the *News-Press* outsider essays assumed sophistication. In 1993, the paper published former marine corps officer David Evans's analysis of domestic job losses following the closure of military bases. Evans, who then worked for Business Executives for National Security, followed up in August

1995 with "Hiroshima Revisited: The Plan to Invade Japan—And Why Truman Dropped the Bomb." (It was published with a photograph of local hardware store executive John Hechinger as a soldier in the Pacific in 1943.) As the new millennium arrived in 2000, Benton mused on who should be "Person of the Century" (perhaps Churchill, perhaps Einstein but probably Franklin Delano Roosevelt).

Candidate endorsements were a staple of *News-Press* editorials. No politician was more regularly backed than then–lieutenant governor and local auto dealership co-owner Don Beyer. Benton, as early as January 1992, called him Virginia's "likely next governor" who "Got a Lot Done in Richmond." (Beyer would lose that bid to Republican Jim Gilmore in 1997.) But when Beyer ran for U.S. Congress beginning in 2014, he could count on *News-Press* backing. When Gilmore was inaugurated in January 1998, reader Ralph McGehee wrote a scathing letter to the editor: "In the entire context of last week's *News-Press*, there was not one mention of the top story in Virginia: The inauguration of Jim Gilmore as Virginia's 68th governor. Mr. Benton, you should take your head out of the sand and try reporting the news again as you used to, then maybe this paper could be taken seriously." Benton would go on to give Gilmore a column (one sample headline from August 2001: "Virginia's in Steady Financial Hands and Sound Financial Shape").

In 2005, a year when the *News-Press* endorsed Richmond mayor Tim Kaine for governor, opponent Jerry Kilgore and his team complained about mistakes in the news coverage of a July debate at the Greenbrier resort. The result: a long, embarrassing list of corrections following a review of the debate transcript to Kilgore's stated positions on restricting abortion and details on the debate's format. In May that year, the *News-Press* published interviews with lieutenant governor candidates Democrat Leslie Byrne (whom it endorsed) and Republican William Bolling (the victor). But its news coverage of the primary drew an angry letter from Ken Sandler of Fairfax, calling its "pro-Byrne" article "a hatchet job" on competing Democrat Chap Petersen. Most *News-Press* endorsements went to Democrats (an exception was Benton's backing of Jeannemarie Devolites Davis for reelection to the state senate in 2007). In May 1998, the paper ran a photograph of Benton with U.S. senator Chuck Robb at the annual Jefferson-Jackson Dinner. But Robb, a former governor, lost to Republican George Allen in 2000.

The first U.S. president elected during the *News-Press*'s tenure, Bill Clinton, won Benton's approval after some initial hesitancy. Coverage in the January 14, 1993 issue featured buzz about whether the newly elected Clinton would imitate Thomas Jefferson and stop in Falls Church on his way from Monticello to his inauguration. (He did not, but he and First Lady Hillary Clinton, in January 1997, attended a Sunday service at Columbia Baptist.) In February, Benton editorialized after the State of the Union Address that the centrist "Clinton has done nothing to earn the trust of the American people." A letter from Dr. Jerome Barret said, "Your editorial shows little evidence that you listened to the president, except with very partisan ears." But by March 1993, Benton was won over after covering a Clinton press conference. "Clinton Downright Presidential Facing White House Press Corps," he wrote in a commentary that August. Though the paper still faulted Clinton for his alleged timidity, the remainder of Clinton's tenure drew sympathetic coverage. "The President's Hand: What It Felt Like" wrote *News-Press* staffer Simon van Steyn after catching up with Clinton at a rally in Springfield, Virginia, and sneaking to the stage. "I couldn't let Nick Benton down."

When the Monica Lewinsky sex scandal broke in 1998, Benton scolded the press for stressing Clinton's imperfections, observing that the president had to deliver his State of the Union Address with news anchors "titillating their imagined audiences with filthy and graphic accounts of sex in the West Wing anteroom." That October, he urged Clinton to focus on using the budget surplus to save Social Security. "Those on both sides, who comply with the wishes of the vast majority of the American people, and put the Lewinsky [affair] behind them, will stand better this November."

In the red-letter election year 2000 (the "tied" election hinged on "hanging chads" in Florida) found Benton posing in August with local Al Gore delegates at George Washington's Mount Vernon. When the race on election night appeared disputably close, his headline read, "Next U.S. President to Win by Margin Far Smaller than Tiny FC." In December, as the litigation and recounts continued, Benton flew to Florida to witness the counting of the chads. Then he ran a photograph of *Bush v. Gore* protestors at the Supreme Court. In the January 25, 2000 issue, he ran a photograph of protesters at Bush's inauguration, headlined "Hail to the Thief."

When former Vermont governor Howard Dean began seeking the Democratic nomination in 2003, his anti-Bush rhetoric drew endorsers early in the primary process. Falls Church's Don Beyer headed a national fundraising effort beginning in June 2003. The paper printed his guest commentary: "Why I Support Howard Dean for President." By November, the Virginia campaign headquarters for Dean had opened its office at 200 Park Avenue, where four hundred gathered for the housewarming.

Surprisingly, Benton himself, in January, was named Dean's coordinator for Falls Church. Dean is "almost like a Falls Church native son," Benton said in an editorial titled "Dean for America." (Other local pols, such as Delegate Jim Scott and Fairfax County supervisors Gerry Connolly and Kate Hanley, backed Democrat John Kerry.) Benton's role as an editor and advocate drew a February 2004 letter from Rick Castelli: "Due to the sacrosanct and independent press, how can Nick be head of Dean campaign, and also offer himself to council candidate." Benton's reply in print read, "It's a fair question. A great deal of thought went into each decision [on how to distinguish] between advocating and accepting a role as a government official....As a newspaperman, I remain first and foremost a citizen, and in editorials and commentaries, I am expected to and have written sharply on behalf of my preferences on political matters."

That August, Dean appeared at Cherry Hill Park, and four thousand witnessed the "Largest Political Assembly Ever Convened in City of Falls Church," the *News-Press* reported with two pages of photographs, one of Dean, Beyer and Benton. Dean "hammered" President Bush for the "insanity" of global unilateralism. But within months, he had been overtaken

In August 2003, Democratic primary presidential candidate Howard Dean attracted the largest crowd in the history of the Falls Church Community Center. *Reuters/Alamy stock photograph.*

by Kerry, who endured Republican attacks that questioned the truthfulness of his tours in Vietnam. Ultimately, Bush won reelection.

When the Barack Obama era began, the *News-Press* was enthused. Watching the first Black president's swearing-in, Benton wrote of an "epochal wallop to the emotional and psychic solar plexus of the nation and the world, myself included, represented by Tuesday's inauguration of President Barack Obama." The next eight years did not dim Benton's approval of the president. And when Obama appeared at nearby Graham Road Elementary School to boost education funding, the paper's headline said, "President Obama Charms Students."

The following cycle, as early as primary season in February 2016, the *News-Press* editorial headline read, "Hillary Clinton for President." "This is a surprisingly easy decision to us," he wrote. "The entire Republican field has shamed and disqualified itself, in our view, with positions and behaviors far more extreme than we've ever seen. Hillary Clinton has a remarkably proven record of achievement over the past two dozen years," he continued. "It surely cannot be lost on anyone the incredible significance of a woman of such achievement and stature becoming the first woman president."

It won't be lost on readers that this was not to be. The Electoral College victory of Donald Trump launched the paper into four years of negative coverage. When Trump wrote a letter attacking Democratic House speaker Nancy Pelosi during his impeachment proceedings in December 2019, Benton wrote of the president's "demented, paranoid mind….It takes all the internalized hate and fear and projects it outward. Everything he is accusing Pelosi of are crimes and excesses his mind is telling him he's guilty of," he wrote. Yet Trump remained popular among most Republicans, who approved of his tax cuts, shrinking of federal agency powers and anti-immigrant rhetoric. Readers of the *News-Press*, nearly two years after Trump left office (and with Trump still claiming his victory was "stolen"), saw the September 2022 headline on a Benton essay, "We're in the Middle of an Ongoing Fascist Coup."

Benton endorsed Joe Biden in his October 23, 2020 editorial as "a solid, reliable choice for a national return to normalcy from the standpoint of a preponderance of both parties." "He's proven it through his long political career, and while there are reasons for almost everyone to be critical…it's all been done with a dignified love of country and the values of democracy."

Benton's forays into national affairs inevitably led him to cover capital city journalism. As a member of the White House Correspondents' Association, he regularly recorded his attendance at the prestigious annual dinner, including getting photographs of himself and his staff in black-tie attire with celebrities such as model Heidi Klum and sex counselor Ruth Westheimer. Falls Church readers, in November 1997, were shown a photograph of CNN's Wolf Blitzer and CBS News's Bill Plante at a White House press conference. In 1998, Benton appeared with Jim Lehrer on PBS NewsHour to discuss presidential politics.

Benton's belief that the news business matters meant he'd run Mike Hoover's coverage of the 1997 opening of the Newseum in Arlington and the awarding of the Pulitzer Prize for photography that year to Falls Church resident Annie Wells. He wrote a tribute to *Washington Post* publisher Katharine Graham following her death in 2001. And when veteran Minnesota journalist and press secretary Al Eisele, who founded *The Hill* publication on Capitol Hill, retired, Benton recruited the Falls Church resident as a freelance writer.

Benton was also skeptical of the downtown media establishment. Early on in his *News-Press* tenure, Benton criticized Clinton for restricting press corps access. A June 4, 1998 editorial titled "Truth and Fairness" chided journalists Claire Shipman and Michael Isikoff for not acknowledging during a panel discussion that the quest for TV ratings affects media coverage. There followed a six-part series titled "Responsible v. Irresponsible Journalism," which bemoaned a drift away from objectivity. During the George W. Bush presidency, Benton complained of national press corps snobbery. "Those of us relegated to sitting in the non-assigned seats at the rear of the cramped White House Press briefing room," he told *Vanity Fair* in the spring of 2003, "or to sit on a window sill or stand along the walls were not only seldom recognized from the podium, but were generally ignored and not infrequently the butt of rude jokes and behavior from the press corps elites."

"The Sorry State of News" was the title of Benton's June 1, 2006 column chiding CNN opinion broadcaster Lou Dobbs for his pro-Bush views. The following April, Benton's column blasted Dobbs directly for his tirades against immigration. "I take it you don't actually watch our broadcast," Dobbs wrote in. "For a columnist writing bemoaning opinion in journalism, you seem utterly indifferent to facts." Benton's reply: "In fact I do watch your program, and I am familiar with how you couch your obsession with immigration policy in the context of the so-called 'war on the middle class.'" Whereas Benton's column was "'clearly delineated as opinion,' by contrast, your hour 'feigns hard news.'"

In April 2000, the *News-Press* reprinted Clinton's upbeat speech on local news to the American Society of Newspaper Editors. But Clinton warned,

"The thing I worry about is that people will have no way of evaluating whether it's true or false."

The *News-Press* is often able to report on overseas wars, terrorism and political strife while providing a local link. "Falls Church Dentist's Saga of Escape from the Mass Murdering Khmer Rouge," read the January 23, 1992 historical report by Catherine Acree. An August 1992 article about five thousand daily deaths from starvation in Somalia, based on local activist Stewart Edwards's hosting of Somalia diplomat Dr. Omar Mohallim, was distributed to the Clinton White House. "Diplomat Killed in Bosnia, Was a Good Neighbor in Falls Church," read the August 1995 coverage of the vehicle crash in Bosnia that killed Ambassador Robert Frasure and two other U.S. officials on a peace mission. The paper's lead story in its January 4, 1996 issue was an interview with a Falls Church civic activist, and it was titled "Challenges of Foreign Service." It was billed as an "Exclusive Interview: Richard McCall's View of the World from the Fifth Floor of the State Department." When Henry Sapalski, the mayor of the Polish city of Bydgoszcz, visited Falls Church in August 1997, Benton ran a photograph of himself with the visitor taken as they discussed the nature of a "responsible free press." The international drama in December 2001—just months after the 9/11 attacks and the United States' invasion of Afghanistan— was that Falls Church native Larry Kaplow was being held at gunpoint in Afghanistan. Just a month later, Afghan president Hamid Karzai, during his visit to Washington, was given a luncheon at the Mustofa Center in nearby Annandale, catered by Panjshir Restaurant owner Aziz Niazy and his daughter, Mastoora. In March 2003, the *News-Press* published an account by city resident Fran Richardson titled "On Life in Cuba Today." When Falls Church, in February 2006, established a sister city relationship with Kokolopori in the Democratic Republic of Congo, the paper followed up the next year by reporting resident William Garvelink's appointment as U.S. ambassador to that nation.

In his commentary, editorials and essays, Benton frequently visited foreign policy topics with no direct link to the Little City. In May 1992, in what he billed as an exclusive with a "U.S. Strategic Policy Expert," he published an interview with Reagan administration negotiator Sven Kraemer: "The Cold War Can't Be Over…If Russian Arms Control Violations Continue." When Israeli prime minister Yitzhak Rabin was assassinated in November 1995, Benton mourned him in an editorial (as he had been on the White House lawn during the signing of the 1993 peace accord between Rabin and PLO leader Yasser Arafat).

News-Press coverage of the Middle East did not always sit well with Falls Churchians. A July 2004 piece on Falls Church native and Jewish American peace activist Jamie Spector, who was being held by Israel for protesting its government's policy, drew criticism in a letter from Beth Heleman, who argued that Spector's International Solidarity Movement was not dedicated to nonviolence as claimed.

And the 2003 U.S. invasion of Iraq to remove Dictator Saddam Hussein drew much criticism in the *News-Press*, along with a controversy that embarrassed local congressman Moran. In the months before the well-telegraphed invasion, Benton's White House column was headlined, "Bush's Cronies Crafted Iraq War Policy Prior to Election," and it questioned the president's motives when he claimed Iraq possessed weapons of mass destruction. In January 2003, the *News-Press* reprinted the text of Senator Ted Kennedy's blast at President Bush's leadership. After Secretary of State Colin Powell made a prowar presentation at the UN that February, Benton's column was headlined, "Powell Sacrifices U.S. Intel Methods and Meaning in Zeal for War." More locally, the paper drew praise in its letters column for its Iraq War coverage, including a survey of Mason High students that showed 63 percent opposed the war.

Longtime congressman Jim Moran regularly marched in the Falls Church Memorial Day parade. *From the* News-Press.

The prowar position would be represented in reprints of *New York Times* columns by David Brooks and by Republican representative Tom Davis, who returned from Iraq with a slideshow for the Falls Church Chamber of Commerce defending U.S. operations there (he would later acknowledge some errors there). But Democratic representative Moran, after visiting Iraq in 2007, believed the United States should get out.

Moran got in hot water in March 2003, when, at a forum in Reston, Virginia, he was asked about the invasion and replied, "If it were not for the strong support of the Jewish community for this war with Iraq, we would not be doing this. The leaders of the Jewish community are influential enough that they could change the direction of where this is going, and I think they should."

Condemnation and charges of anti-Semitism rained in from editorial pages (particularly from the *Washington Post*) and Jewish activists. Delegate Hull withdrew his support for Moran. But Benton editorialized in defense of the lawmaker, offering a list of Jewish leaders who'd come forward with views that neither Moran nor the *News-Press* are anti-Semitic.

Moran would go on to win reelection, telling the *News-Press*, "We need to be careful about being defensive about being liberals....Liberalism is the essence of human progress."

18

In Memoriam

Obituaries and news write-ups of tragic, sudden deaths inescapably form a key plank of a local paper's compact with readers. It is a sad but must-do beat. The *News-Press*, over the years, managed to regularly break such stories, document the deaths of local personalities and even keep up with the passing of former city residents who were still recalled by many. The following are a sampling:

> June 1991: Mary Lee Tatum, a sex education teacher in Falls Church schools, dies in auto accident at fifty-six.

> January 1995: Stewart Edwards, a founder of the Falls Church Citizens Organization and "friend of the *News-Press*," dies at seventy-six.

> March 1995: Palestinian American Issa Khalil Ayoub, founder of Charlie's Pizza, dies at sixty-seven.

> July 1995, front-page headline: "Popular Local Teen Dies in Horseback Riding Fall," George Mason High School student Maria Nudell, at fourteen. Her parents thank Benton in the next issue for his editorial.

> October 1996: Larry Graves, a representative of the National Newspaper Association and beloved soccer coach, dies. A park was later named for him.

Murphy's has been a fixture on West Broad Street and in Arlington since its founding in 1965. *Author's photograph.*

August 1997, lead story headline: "Margaret Jones, Falls Church's Pre-eminent 'World Citizen' Dies" at seventy-six. Editorial cites her presidency of the League of Women Voters and states that she ran a model United Nations at George Mason High School. She also wrote columns and proofread at the *News-Press*.

September 1997: Ruth Checknoff, a science teacher and chair of city's Senior Commission, dies at seventy-one.

October 1997: "City Father" Hal Silverstein dies at eighty. He was a city councilman for twelve years and was honored by the Village Preservation and Improvement Society as the "spirit of Falls Church."

May 1998: Former sheriff John H. Martin dies in Florida. He served for thirty years until 1992.

August 1999: Wayne Sanford, a head of local Republicans, former CIA operative and Marine veteran of World War II, dies at eighty.

September 1999: Nancy Beyer, mother of Volvo dealership owner Mike Beyer and Congressman Don Beyer, dies at seventy-three. Her husband, Don Sr., died in December 2017 at the age of ninety-three.

May 25, 2000: Hannah Knudsen, a fifth grader at Thomas Jefferson Elementary, dies after her bicycle was struck by a minivan at Robinson Place and Rosemary Lane. Separately, Robert Kett, a computer consultant and school volunteer, dies of cancer at thirty-nine.

July 2000: Roger Wollenberg, an attorney, school board member and a founder of Citizens for a Better City, dies at eighty-one.

August 2000: Edna Clark, the first woman elected to city council and former president of the chamber of commerce, dies at eighty-five.

November 2000: David Steinberg, the co-owner and renovator of State Theatre, dies in his sleep at forty-three in Washington, D.C., after the theater had "just begun to hit its stride." Separately, Linwood "Lin" Lemon, a 1969 graduate of George Mason High School, dies at fifty of heart attack while playing basketball in Glen Allen, Virginia.

February 2001: James E. Anderson, a lifelong Falls Churchian and the founder of Anderson Moving and Storage, dies at eighty-eight.

March 2001: Franklin Day, a George Mason High School '96 graduate and student at Colgate University, dies at twenty-three of leukemia.

June 2001: Abigail Burroughs, a George Mason High School graduate who battled cancer and drug companies in search of experimental drugs, dies at twenty-one at the University of Virginia. Her courage inspired a scholarship fund in her memory. Separately, Edith Abramson, a "Major Influence in Founding of CBC Here" and a PTA and Democratic Party activist, dies at eighty-two.

July 2001: Stephen Gordon, the founder of Falls Church Computer and "Soccer Dad Extraordinaire," dies at forty-one from cancer and liver failure.

October 2001: Jane Dexter, a former student activist for Falls Church City Public Schools, president of the League of Women Voters and sole woman on the school board from 1954 to 1966, dies at eighty-two. Separately, former Falls Church revenue commissioner Claude Wells, the brother of Harry Wells, dies at eighty-eight.

August 2002: Dan Herlinger, a *Washington Post* staffer and "neighborhood icon" who watched world from his wheelchair at the corner of Timber and Park Lanes, dies.

February 2002: Falls Church native and business leader William C. Shreve Jr., a chamber of commerce leader and housing executive (*News-Press* landlord) with lineage back to the American Revolution, dies in his sleep at fifty-nine.

March 2002: Former city police dispatcher Carol Hilleary, who worked for ten years at the Animal Welfare League of Arlington, dies at forty-two of cancer.

August 2002: Montie Cone, who served on Falls Church Planning Commission and helped plan the Metro stop in the 1970s, dies at ninety-five.

January 2003: Owen Jones, who, during the 1960s, was president of Village Preservation and Improvement Society, dies at ninety-seven, having lost two children, whom he raised in Falls Church, to car accidents.

June 2003: Nan Netherton, a Falls Church–based, award-winning historian of Northern Virginia, dies at seventy-seven.

July 2003: Carol Fellman, who worked for twenty-two years in Falls Church schools as the secretary to the middle school principal, dies of cancer.

November 2003: Stephen A. Benton, a pioneer in holography, professor at Massachusetts Institute of Technology and brother of *News-Press* owner, dies of brain cancer at sixty-one.

September 2004: Harry E. Wells, "The Man They Named Falls Church City Hall After Dies at Age 87." He had been a city employee since 1948 and spent years as the city manager.

January 2005: Beverly Burns, a former League of Women Voters president, dies at seventy-six.

February 2005: Jim Elkin, an optician and three-term chamber of commerce chief, dies at sixty-seven.

April 2005: Stephen Kuhn, a construction supervisor for Carr Companies, dies at fifty-four of heart attack while playing basketball at the community center. His two daughters with his wife, Cynthia Goodrich, played basketball for George Mason High School.

June 2005: Arlington Resurrection Lutheran pastor Melvin Lange dies at ninety-four. Separately, ex–police chief Kenneth Johnson dies at sixty-seven.

January 2006: Robert McAllister, the chair of the Falls Church Military History Forum, dies at eighty-two.

March 2006: Chauncey Levy, an ophthalmologist married to art instructor and *News-Press* columnist Eileen Levy, dies at seventy-nine. (Eileen died in February 2023.)

May 2006: Nora Hempill, a student publications editor and cheerleader at George Mason High School and a University of Virginia student, dies of cancer at nineteen. Separately, two city employees, Timothy and Cynthia Hohner, die at forty-seven in a bicycle accident.

June 2006: Valerie Stanley, a library aide and beloved children's storyteller, dies at seventy-seven.

July 2006: Charles Hedetniemi, a technical editor, city councilman and charter member of Citizens for a Better City, dies at ninety-one.

August 2006: Robert Herndon, a longtime Rotary Club president and air force career veteran, dies at eighty-nine. Separately, Clifford A. Thorpe, a publisher of the Professional Surveyor, dies at ninety.

October 2006: Patrick Gibbon, a Falls Church native and Virginia Commonwealth University psychology student, dies at twenty-one.

December 2006: Jerry Ziskind, for eighteen years a popular elementary school teacher, dies at sixty-three.

April 2007: Sonny Warner, a blues recording artist and guitarist born in Falls Church who performed at Cherry Hill, dies at seventy-seven.

November 2007: John Scanlon, a Falls Church councilman and U.S. ambassador in the Foreign Service, dies at seventy-nine.

December 2007: Peter Rose, who worked for thirty-two years as a Falls Church teacher, dies of cancer at fifty-seven.

July 2009: Bob Morrison, who was elected four times as Falls Church treasurer (1993–2006) and a friend of the *News-Press* and, later, a professional photographer, dies from colon cancer at seventy-one.

May 2010: Ross Netherton, a city resident and longtime Northern Virginia historian and author, dies at ninety-five.

June 2010: Walter Herbert Morse, a member and chairman of Falls Church City School Board (1969–77) and Sunday school supervisor at Falls Church Episcopal Church, dies at ninety. Separately, Carey Rainey Gray, a reading specialist at Thomas Jefferson Elementary, dies of cancer at thirty-four.

January 2011: Margaret Moses Dale, a coproprietor of the city's Dale Lumber Co. from the 1950s until it moved from Gordon Road to Fairfax Station, dies in the hospital in Leesburg, Virginia.

November 2011: Richard "Jack" Marsh, a George Mason High School athlete, dies suddenly from complications of a heart-lung disorder. A standing room–only memorial service was held in the school auditorium.

April 2012: Marie Hirst Yochim, the former president general of the Daughters of the American Revolution whose family resided for ten generations in Falls Church (her nephew was city historian Melvin Steadman), dies at Arlington's Virginia Hospital Center at ninety-two.

July 2012: David Minton, a former U.S. Postal Service Commission executive director and Falls Church councilman (1990–94), dies in Denton, Texas, at seventy-seven.

August 2012: Robert Greene Turner, a past member of the Falls Church School Board credited with generating the impetus for the formation of the nonprofit Falls Church Education Foundation, dies at seventy-one.

November 2012: Ed Strait, a city council member, community activist and federal budget officer, dies at eighty-eight.

August 2013: James Longo Jr., a George Mason High School class of 1994 graduate, dies of a self-inflicted gunshot wound.

May 2014: Stephen Sprague, a director at the U.S. Housing and Urban Development Department, community activist and treasurer of Citizens for a Better City, dies at sixty-nine.

July 2015: W. John Cameron, a transportation consultant and member of the Falls Church City Council and Planning Commission in the early 1980s, dies at a hospital in Durham, North Carolina, at seventy-four.

February 2016: Samuel Waters, a stage singer at George Mason High School (class of 2011) who wrote personal essays for the *News-Press*, dies of cancer at twenty-two.

October 2016: John Wells, an adult education entrepreneur, air force veteran who served in Vietnam and a Falls Church scouting leader, dies at eighty-two. Separately, Andrew Upshur, a delivery man for the U.S. Postal Service, serving Falls Church City, dies.

November 2017: Chris Bergin, the president of Falls Church–based Tax Analysts and former chamber of commerce president, dies at sixty-five following complications from surgery.

February 2019: Gary LaPorta, a Revenue Commission employee who co-owned Miniatures from the Attic with his wife, June, dies at seventy-two.

The historic Oakwood Cemetery, dating before the Civil War, is the final resting place of many prominent Falls Churchians and Arlingtonians. *Author's photograph.*

June 2020: Barbara Cram, a much-awarded citizen volunteer, Greenscape gardening shop owner and local arts promoter, dies at seventy-three. The city council proclaimed Thursday, May 28, 2020, the first-ever Barbara Cram Day in the City of Falls Church.

June 2021: Al Eisele, a journalist, founder of *The Hill* newspaper and vice-presidential press secretary for Walter Mondale, dies at the age of eighty-five.

December 2022: Edna Nina Frady, a local Democratic Party leader nicknamed "Boss Frady" who was known to statewide politicians, dies at ninety at Goodwin House in Falls Church. The daughter of city father Donald Frady was a member of the Falls Church Women's Club, the Village Preservation and Improvement Society and Citizens for a Better City.

February 2023: Merelyn Kaye, a major real estate agent and sixty-year resident who worked with the Village Preservation and Improvement Society, the Victorian Society of Falls Church and Historic Falls Church Inc., dies at age eighty-five.

Epilogue

After thirty-three years and more than 1,700 issues—without missing a weekly deadline—the *Falls Church News-Press* is woven into the fabric of the Little City. The community *did* move on editor Nick Benton's urging that it embrace denser commercial development to produce revenue for top-quality schools. American society *did* evolve toward greater acceptance of the gay community. The 2003 invasion of Iraq *does* appear to most, in retrospect, to have been a mistake, and President Donald Trump *is* indeed unlikely to be looked upon favorably by history. Those were all in line with the Bentonian worldview. True, Benton didn't get the affordable housing he recommended, nor the minor-league ball team he rooted for. Nor did his editorials succeed in electing Howard Dean, Al Gore, John Kerry or Hillary Clinton to the White House.

The *News-Press* continues melding traditional newspapering with a dose of the avant-garde. But for most readers, it feels like home. And though Benton, by far, has written the lion's share of its copy, the paper would not have lasted decades without a dedicated odd-hours staff. Their endurance reflects Benton's vision and skills as a talent spotter and nurturer—and his thick skin. The paper survived as a feat of determination in a climate unfriendly to independent local news.

This author's year spent reading back issues revealed a steady inflow of reader praise, offset by some intelligent, if occasionally harsh, backtalk. A sampling: "To me," wrote Ron Crouch in August 1993, "the true value of the *FCNP* is not just in providing unbiased information but as a positive

The modestly sized but ambitious *News-Press* staff at work during a Wednesday production day in 2022. *Author's photograph.*

influence and the source of sharing all those good and happy things that occur or happen to my fellow citizens."

The weekly was heralded as a "great builder of community," in February 1994 by Cheryl Dimon. "I do not always agree with the views stated within, but I enjoy learning about 'the other side' and I commend you highly for providing a civilized forum for the exchange of ideas."

After a tough council election campaign, Falls Church Community Organization members Mary Ann Capria, Greg Brown and Sam Mabry wrote, "Our heartfelt thanks to Nick Benton, who has worked so hard for so long to encourage economic development. Without the *News-Press*, the city would lack political dynamism with the consequent diminished possibility for future growth and maturity."

A different message came in the April 19, 2001 issue from Sergio Cueto: "Your last editorial is way off. First you need to get past your '60s ideas and come to the 21st century....Benton should visit some of Falls Church's blue-collar population who can't afford a tax hike." He continued, "You are surrounded by people of wealth and politics."

Flash forward to the December 5, 2002 issue: "How dare you insult our elected officials," charged Jeannine Small. "Since you seem to know the solutions to all problems, perhaps you should run for office."

Councilman David Snyder wrote in the April 3, 2003 issue, "While I don't always agree with the *News-Press*, I am thankful it is here." That November,

Jacksonville, Florida teacher Pat Lewis said reading the paper is "the highlight of the week," since her mother, Jean Skillman of Falls Church, mails it down so she can share it with students.

But in January 2005, Trina Erhard wrote that she had been "hoping to find one article not written by someone who is anything but a left-leaning, liberal." So, she throws her copy away. (Benton's reply pointed to the columns by conservative *New York Times* columnist William Safire.) Rick Munoz suggested that February: "I wish you folks at the *News-Press* would stop printing your 'platform'—which includes such lofty goals as never mixing news and editorial policy—when every week's edition routinely flouts that noble aim."

Benton's unique project also drew plaudits, with qualifications, from prominent readers and associates interviewed in 2022.

Former managing editor Jody Fellows, the longest serving *News-Press* staffer, said, "Nick is a great mentor, though not very hands-on. But I learned a lot from observing him. He's very set in his ideology and ways. I didn't agree with all of it, but it's his paper. Still, I was one of the few people who could confront him and say, 'Hey, not right, maybe we shouldn't do this.' In the end, Nick is very dedicated to what he believes in, stands by it and doesn't waver."

In the 1990s, the paper flew its banner on the West Broad Street office. *From the* News-Press.

Accountant and friend Mike Diener said the "newspaper has a lot of power and you can use it to do some good work. But it didn't always succeed. Nick was always open to doing the right thing and publicizing it, and without Nick's support these things wouldn't have happened. It's not just a strategy— he really believed. Nick is not the easiest person to approach, but he has a huge heart."

Councilman Phil Duncan, a retired journalist, said "a printed newspaper is a glue for the community and is not like any other means of conveying information. Whoever runs it, I don't begrudge them their opinions. It's such hard work, I give deference to them."

In a 2021 company history, Benton declared:

> *The past 30 years have been far and away the happiest and most fulfilling of my life. It has not always been sweetness and light, as an independent newspaper and opinionated editor must expect to take the brunt of a lot of disdain from those who don't always agree with it. But that is far more than offset by the unexpected kindness and appreciation often expressed by complete strangers in a check-out line at a local supermarket, for example, and the satisfaction of knowing one is doing one's best to provide a vital public service. I am confident the newspaper has accumulated far more fans than detractors.*

Index

About the Author

Charlie Clark, a retired journalist, has written three other local history books: *Arlington County Chronicles*, *Hidden History of Arlington County* and *Lost Arlington County*, all published by The History Press. In 2021, he published the first full biography of George Washington Parke Custis, an undersung "child of Mount Vernon," with McFarland Books. A native of Arlington, Virginia, he continues to write the weekly "Our Man in Arlington" column for the *Falls Church News-Press*. In July 2019, he retired as a senior correspondent for Government Executive Media Group. He previously worked as an editor or writer for the *Washington Post*, *Congressional Quarterly*, *National Journal*, Time-Life Books, Tax Analysts and the Association of Governing Boards of Universities and Colleges.

Visit us at
www.historypress.com
....